The Side Income Playbook

Turning Skills You Already Have Into a Second Income Stream Without Quitting Your Job

Daniel Cross

First edition, 2026

Published by Daniel Cross

This book is intended for general educational and reflective purposes only. It is not a substitute for professional financial, legal, medical, or mental health advice, diagnosis, or treatment. Always seek the advice of a qualified professional with any questions regarding your specific circumstances. Never disregard professional advice or delay seeking it because of something you have read in this book. Names and identifying details in any illustrative examples are anonymous/archetypal composites, not depictions of a single real individual.

Contents

Foreword

The first side income I ever built was fixing other people's spreadsheets. Not designing anything, not consulting in the way that word gets used now — I sat with a coworker's broken formulas after hours and untangled them for twenty dollars a pop, because I was fast at it and she'd have paid someone anyway. It never became a business. I didn't know that was a possible outcome at the time. I thought of it as a favor with a price tag on it, did maybe a dozen of them over two years, and let it die quietly when I changed jobs and lost the referral chain that fed it.

Looking back, everything that would have turned that into something durable was sitting right there. I had a skill someone would pay for. I had proof people would actually pay for it — a dozen transactions is proof, not a hunch. What I didn't have was a system: no clear offer, no repeatable way to find the next client, no idea what to charge beyond whatever felt fair in the moment, and no plan for what happened after the favor. I let the whole thing run on improvisation, and improvisation doesn't compound. A system does.

This book is what I wish I'd had instead. It isn't about finding your passion, and it isn't about hustle as an identity — I don't think either does much for a person sitting at a kitchen table on a Tuesday night, trying to figure out whether the thing they're good at could actually turn into money without blowing up their day job. What helps is mechanics: how to spot the offer hiding inside a skill you already have, how to price it the first time with no track record to point to, how to find a first client without cold-calling strangers, how to keep the IRS satisfied without an accountant you can't afford yet, and how to be honest about when a side income can realistically replace a primary one.

None of this requires quitting anything. Most of it requires two or three hours a week, applied with a plan instead of at random, the way I applied mine. I got twelve spreadsheet jobs and a shrug. You can do better than that, and this book is the difference between the two.

— Daniel Cross

Introduction — How to Use This Book

This book has one job: to take a skill you already have and turn it into money that shows up on a schedule, without asking you to leave the job that currently pays your bills. That's the whole promise. It isn't a book about finding a calling, and it isn't a book about hustle culture — you won't find advice in here about waking up at 4:30 a.m. or grinding until you collapse. What you'll find is a set of mechanical steps: how to identify what's actually sellable in what you already know, how to price it the first time, how to get a first client without a marketing budget or an audience, how to protect the job you still need while you build the thing that might eventually replace it, and how to handle the boring but consequential parts — business structure, quarterly taxes, and the decision of when to pay yourself versus when to put money back into the business.

Every chapter in this book follows the same shape:

The situation — a realistic scenario, built from the recognizable shape of a common starting point rather than a single real person's exact story. No names, no case studies you're meant to recognize — just the pattern, because the pattern is what repeats.

The mechanics — what's actually happening underneath the situation. Why the obvious move often fails, where the real leverage sits, and what changes the outcome.

The script or framework — a concrete tool. A worksheet, a formula, an actual message you can send today, a decision tree you can run against your own numbers.

A worked example — the tool in motion, start to finish, so you can see the shape of it rather than just the theory.

You don't need to read this book cover to cover before doing anything. If you already know what skill you're building an offer around, skip to Chapter 2. If you have an offer but no idea what to charge, start at Chapter 3. If pricing is settled and the problem is finding someone willing to pay it, Chapter 4 is built for exactly that moment. If you're already earning something and the paperwork is starting to feel like a liability, Chapters 6 and 7 handle structure and taxes in the order most people actually need them. And if the real question keeping you up is whether this could ever become your whole income, Chapter 10 gives you the arithmetic to answer that honestly instead of guessing.

A note on the scenarios throughout this book: every situation described — the teacher, the technician, the driver, the paralegal — is a composite, built from the common shape of how a side income actually starts, not a record of one real person's exact circumstances. If one of them lands close to your own life, that's not a coincidence. It's meant to.

A note on numbers, too. Dollar figures, tax rates, and specific thresholds appear throughout as illustrations of a mechanism, not as claims about current law or current market rates. Tax brackets, self-employment tax rates, and safe-harbor thresholds are set by the IRS and do change — verify the current figures at irs.gov before filing anything, using the sources listed at the back of this book as your starting point. What doesn't change is the logic: why quarterly taxes exist, why a sole proprietorship behaves differently from an LLC, why a first price should be set the way Chapter 3 describes. That logic is the actual content of this book. The specific numbers in the examples are there to make it concrete, not to be copied into your own return.

One last thing, because it matters more than anything else in this introduction: this book assumes you have real hours available outside your job — evenings, weekends, a lunch break, whatever your specific situation allows — and it assumes you're not already stretched past the point where adding anything would cost you your health or your primary job's performance. If that's genuinely your situation right now, the honest answer is that this isn't the season to start a side income, and no framework in this book changes that math. For everyone else, with real if limited hours to work with, everything that follows is built to make those hours count.

A word, too, on why the chapters run in this specific order. The sequence isn't arbitrary — it follows the actual order most side incomes need to solve their problems in, from first principles to eventual scale. You can't price an offer you haven't built yet, which is why pricing sits in Chapter 3, after the skill inventory and offer-building of Chapters 1 and 2. You can't sensibly worry about business structure or quarterly taxes before you have a client, which is why acquisition sits in Chapter 4, ahead of the paperwork chapters. And the honest math of a full income replacement in Chapter 10 only means anything once real, sustained revenue exists to run the calculation against, which is why it closes the book rather than opening it. Reading out of order is entirely fine once you know where you actually are — the map above exists for exactly that — but the order itself reflects the real sequence a side income tends to move through, and it's worth understanding that sequence even if your own path through it isn't strictly linear.

This book also makes a deliberate choice about what it doesn't cover, and that choice is worth stating up front rather than leaving readers to wonder why a familiar topic is missing. It doesn't cover finding your passion or deciding what kind of work would make you happy — that's real, worthwhile territory, and other books cover it well, but it isn't this book's job. It doesn't cover building a large-scale personal brand or a public following, which is a legitimate long-term asset but a slow, uncertain first move for someone trying to land a first paying client this month. And it doesn't cover venture-style business building — raising outside capital, building a large team, chasing rapid scale — because that's a different kind of business entirely, with a different risk profile and a different playbook, from the specific, self-funded, spare-hours side income this book is built around.

Chapter 1 — What You Already Have Is Probably Sellable

Why a skill inventory beats a "find your passion" exercise

The situation

A high school biology teacher spends three unpaid hours every August rebuilding her lesson plans from scratch, because the district's curriculum changes just enough each year that last year's material doesn't quite fit. She's good at this in a way that goes beyond just being a competent teacher — she can take a dense unit on cellular respiration and turn it into something a fifteen-year-old will actually sit still for, complete with pacing, worksheets, and the kind of formative-assessment questions that catch confusion before a test does. Colleagues ask to borrow her materials constantly. She's never once considered that this specific skill — not "teaching" broadly, but this exact, narrow ability to structure a unit — might be worth money to someone outside her own building.

This is the most common blind spot at the start of any side income: the belief that what you're good at doesn't count as a skill unless it's rare, credentialed, or already attached to a job title like "consultant" or "freelancer." It almost never works that way. The things people pay for are usually narrower and more specific than a job title, and they're frequently things the person doing them has stopped noticing entirely, because doing them well has become invisible to the person doing it.

The mechanics

There's a reliable pattern in how people misjudge their own sellable skills, and it runs in a consistent direction: broad, generic self-descriptions ("I'm organized," "I'm good with people," "I know a lot about computers") feel true but don't translate into an offer, while narrow, specific capabilities ("I can take a messy 40-person event's logistics and build a run-of-show that survives contact with reality," "I can look at three months of a small business's bank statements and tell you where the money's actually going") translate immediately, because they describe a concrete outcome someone else can picture themselves needing.

The reason broad self-descriptions don't sell is simple: nobody buys "organized." They buy a specific problem solved. A skill only becomes an offer once it's been narrowed down to the point where a stranger can hear it and immediately think of a moment in their own life when they needed exactly that. This is the entire mechanical difference between a side income that gets started and one that stays a vague intention for years — not talent, not market demand, but specificity.

There's a second pattern to flag here too: the skills most available for a side income usually aren't the ones from your job title. They're the adjacent skills you built as a side effect of doing your actual job well — the teacher's unit-planning ability sitting inside "teacher," the warehouse supervisor's scheduling instinct sitting inside "supervisor," the nurse's gift for calming down a frightened patient's family sitting inside "nurse." These adjacent skills are frequently more sellable than the primary job skill, precisely because they're rarer outside the context that produced them, and because the person who has them has almost never thought to separate them out and look at them on their own.

There's a third mechanical point worth understanding before running the exercise below: the reason this identification step gets skipped so often isn't laziness — it's that a skill genuinely becomes invisible to the person who has it. Psychologists call a version of this the curse of knowledge: once something has become automatic, it's genuinely hard to remember what it felt like not to know it, which makes it hard to recognize as a skill at all rather than just "how things are." This is why the raw-list exercise in this chapter deliberately asks for outcomes rather than self-assessment — "I can take a messy budget spreadsheet and turn it into something a non-numbers person can actually read in five minutes" surfaces evidence a person can check against their own memory, where "I'm good with numbers" only asks them to trust a vague self-rating they've likely never actually tested.

It's also worth being honest about why the "find your passion" framing that's common in general career advice fails specifically at this stage, and why this book deliberately avoids it. Passion is a genuine, valuable thing in a career or a creative pursuit, but it's a poor filter for a first side-income offer, because passion and market demand are only loosely correlated, and a first-time side income needs demand more urgently than it needs deep personal meaning. The four-step process in this chapter is built to surface what's sellable first — genuine interest still matters, which is why Step 4 explicitly checks for it, but it's the third filter applied, not the first, precisely because leading with passion alone is how so many side-income attempts stall out chasing an idea nobody was actually paying for.

The script and framework

Step 1 — Build a raw list, not a filtered one. Set a timer for fifteen minutes and write down everything you're meaningfully better at than an average person, without filtering for whether it "counts." Include job skills, but push past them into adjacent ones: what do people ask you to help with informally? What have you gotten faster or better at without meaning to? What do you notice that other people in your same role seem to miss? Write in full sentences describing an outcome, not single words — not "writing," but "I can take a rambling first draft and cut it down to something that actually holds a reader's attention."

Step 2 — Run each item through the Stranger Test. For each item on your list, ask: if I described this to a stranger at a party, would they be able to picture a specific moment in their own life or business where this would have helped them? "I'm good with people" fails this test — it's too vague to picture. "I can walk into a chaotic small retail store's back office and build an inventory system that actually gets used" passes it easily, because the listener can picture the mess in their own head immediately.

Step 3 — Cross-reference against evidence you already have. For every item that passes the Stranger Test, write down the actual evidence you have that you're good at it — not credentials, evidence. Times you've done it. Results you produced. Compliments you've gotten unprompted, which are a more honest signal than compliments you fished for. This step matters because the offer you eventually build in Chapter 2 needs a story behind it, and the story needs to be true.

Step 4 — Rank what's left by two questions: do you actually want to do more of this, and does it fit inside the hours you actually have. A skill can pass the Stranger Test and still be wrong for a side income if doing more of it would make you miserable, or if it structurally requires hours you don't have — a skill that only works during weekday business hours is a poor match for someone whose only free time is evenings and weekends. Cross those off, even if they're your most impressive skill. The best side-income skill is the one that's sellable, true, wanted, and schedule-compatible, all four at once — not just the most impressive one on paper.

If this four-step process produces no single obvious winner on the first pass, that's normal rather than a sign the exercise failed — run it again a week later, after paying deliberate attention in the meantime to moments when someone asks for your help, compliments something you did without prompting, or you notice yourself doing something faster or better than the people around you. A second pass, informed by even a week of paying real attention to these small signals, routinely surfaces items the first pass missed entirely, simply because the first pass has to work from memory alone and the second gets to work from a week of fresh, specific evidence.

Worked example

The biology teacher runs her raw list and comes up with eleven items, most of them vague — "communication," "patience," "knowledge of science." Buried in the middle of the list, in more specific language, is: "I can take a dense, disorganized state curriculum standard and turn it into a week of lesson plans that actually keep a room of teenagers engaged." She runs it through the Stranger Test and it passes immediately — any new teacher, any homeschooling parent, any small private-school administrator can instantly picture needing exactly that.

Her evidence: colleagues have borrowed her materials for six years running, unprompted. A department head once asked her to run a lunch-and-learn for newer teachers on unit pacing. She's never been paid for any of it, but the demand has always been there, informally, for free.

She checks it against wants and hours: she genuinely likes building the materials — it's the part of teaching she'd do even without being asked — and it fits her actual available hours, since most of the work happens in blocks she already protects for lesson planning anyway, just with a slightly wider scope.

Everything else on her list gets set aside for now, not because it's untrue but because this is the one that's sellable, true, wanted, and schedule-compatible all at once. That specific, narrow skill — not "teaching," but structured unit-planning for a specific subject and grade band — becomes the raw material for the offer she builds in the next chapter.

A second worked example

An IT help desk technician runs the same exercise and lands on something he'd never thought to separate from his job title: he's unusually good at writing troubleshooting instructions that non-technical people can actually follow without calling back confused twenty minutes later. His raw list starts with "I know computers," which fails the Stranger Test outright — it's too broad to picture. Pushed further, it narrows to "I can take a repeated tech-support problem and write a short, plain-language guide that lets someone fix it themselves the first time," which passes immediately, because anyone who's ever called a help desk can picture wanting exactly that.

His evidence: his own team's internal knowledge base, which he rewrote unofficially over a year because the original documentation kept generating repeat tickets, and which measurably cut his team's call volume on the topics he rewrote. He checks it against wants and hours — he genuinely enjoys the writing part of his job more than the phone part, and it fits easily into evening hours since it requires no live availability at all — and settles on plain-language technical documentation, for small businesses too small to have their own technical writer, as his specific, narrow, evidenced skill.

Frequently misunderstood point: a skill inventory isn't the same as a resume

It's easy to run the exercise in this chapter the way you'd update a resume — listing job titles, credentials, and responsibilities — and come away with a list that's technically accurate and almost entirely useless for building an offer. A resume is written for someone screening you against a role you're applying for; it rewards breadth and credentials. A skill inventory for a side income is written to surface a narrow, specific, provable outcome a stranger would pay for on its own, disconnected from any job title at all. The two documents can share source material, but they're built for different purposes, and running this chapter's exercise with a resume mindset is the most common reason people finish it with a list that reads impressively and sells nothing.

A note on skills that feel "too basic to sell"

The most common objection at this stage isn't "I don't have any skills" — it's "the thing I'm good at is too basic to be worth money to anyone." This is worth taking seriously and dismissing at the same time. It's worth taking seriously because the feeling is genuine and common. It's worth dismissing because "basic to you" and "basic to your buyer" are two entirely different measurements, and the gap between them is exactly where a side income lives. A skill feels basic when you've done it so many times it's become automatic — but automatic-to-you is frequently rare-and-valuable-to-someone-who's-never-done-it-before. The person drowning in a chaotic spreadsheet doesn't care that untangling formulas is "basic" to you. They care that it's currently costing them hours they don't have, and you can fix it in twenty minutes.

Common objections and how to handle them

"What if I list my skills and nothing passes the Stranger Test?" This happens less often than people expect, and when it does, it's usually a symptom of writing the raw list in Step 1 too abstractly rather than a real absence of sellable ability. Go back to the raw list and rewrite each vague item as a specific outcome — not "I'm good at cooking" but "I can plan and execute a dinner for twelve without anyone in the kitchen feeling like a guest." Almost every genuinely vague item has a specific version hiding underneath it; the exercise is finding that version, not proving the item doesn't exist.

"What if the skill I'm most excited about isn't the one that tests best?" This is common, and it's worth resisting the urge to force the exciting-but-untested skill into the offer anyway. A skill that fails the Stranger Test isn't necessarily worthless — it might just need a narrower, more specific framing than you've tried yet, or it might genuinely need more evidence behind it before it's ready to sell. Either way, start with whichever skill is sellable, true, wanted, and schedule-compatible right now, and treat the exciting-but-unready one as a second offer to develop later, once the first one has taught you the mechanics of running a side income at all.

"What if I have too many things that pass the test and can't choose?" A good problem to have, and the fix is simple: pick the one with the strongest existing evidence from Step 3, not the one that sounds most impressive in the abstract. Evidence you already have is worth more at this stage than potential you haven't demonstrated yet, because it shortens the distance to Chapter 2's offer-building step and Chapter 4's first-client search.

Adapting the inventory across different kinds of jobs

The four-step process in this chapter works the same way regardless of profession, but where the sellable skill tends to hide varies by the shape of the job it's coming from. In hands-on trades and physical work, the sellable skill is frequently a specific technique or shortcut that took years to develop and now looks effortless — the exact kind of thing that fails the Stranger Test when described as "I'm experienced" and passes easily when described as the specific outcome that experience produces. In office and administrative roles, the sellable skill often hides in whatever informal role you've taken on beyond your job description — the person everyone asks to fix the shared calendar, write the tricky email, or untangle the confusing process nobody documented. In caregiving and service roles — teaching, healthcare support, hospitality — the sellable skill is frequently a specific way of handling a difficult moment with another person that colleagues have noticed and remarked on, even if it's never been named directly as a skill at all. In every case, the direction to search is the same: toward the specific, evidenced, adjacent capability, not toward the job title itself.

Warning signs you're about to skip this chapter's actual work

A few patterns worth checking yourself against before moving forward, since they tend to repeat regardless of the specific skill involved. You're already imagining a fully built offer and a first client before you've written a single item on the raw list — that's skipping ahead past the evidence-gathering this chapter exists to force. You're dismissing an item on your list as "not a real skill" without running it through the Stranger Test first — that's judgment substituting for the actual exercise. You're gravitating toward the most impressive-sounding item on your list rather than the one with the strongest real evidence behind it — that's optimizing for how the choice sounds out loud rather than for what's most likely to actually convert into a first paying client. Any of these three patterns showing up is a cue to slow down and run the actual steps in order, rather than skipping to a conclusion the exercise was supposed to produce.

A short exercise before you move to Chapter 2

Take the raw list from Step 1 and, next to each item that survived the Stranger Test, write one real sentence of evidence — a specific instance, not a general impression of yourself. Then circle the single item with the strongest evidence, the clearest schedule fit, and the most genuine interest, all three at once. That circled item is what the rest of this book is built around. Everything from here forward — the offer, the price, the outreach, the time-boxing — works better when it's aimed at one specific, well-evidenced skill rather than a blurred combination of several.

Building the inventory across a nontraditional or varied career

The exercise in this chapter assumes a certain simplicity — one current job, one clear set of skills sitting inside it — that doesn't match everyone's actual work history. If your career has moved across several unrelated jobs, included stretches of unpaid caregiving, or mixed formal employment with informal or gig work, the raw-list exercise still works, but it benefits from a small adjustment: instead of building the list from your current job alone, build it from every meaningful stretch of work or responsibility you've held, treating each one as its own separate source rather than trying to force them into a single unified narrative.

A person who spent four years managing a retail team, then two years doing informal bookkeeping for a family member's small business, then a year as a full-time caregiver for an aging parent has three genuinely distinct sources to draw from, each with its own adjacent skills worth surfacing — the retail years might surface a gift for de-escalating an upset customer calmly, the bookkeeping years might surface a real facility with reading a small business's cash flow at a glance, and the caregiving years might surface an unusually calm, organized way of managing a complex, ever-changing schedule of appointments and medications under real pressure. None of these needs to connect neatly to the others, and none needs to connect to what you're doing for income right now. The Stranger Test and the evidence-check from Steps 2 and 3 apply identically regardless of where in your history the skill was built — what matters is that the evidence is real and specific, not that the skill traces back to your most recent or most prominent job title.

This matters particularly for anyone who's spent a stretch of time outside traditional paid employment entirely — full-time parenting, caregiving, a medical leave, a period between jobs — since it's common to undervalue exactly this kind of experience simply because it never came with a paycheck attached. A parent who's spent three years coordinating a household's schedules, budgets, and logistics has very often built exactly the kind of organizational skill that sells well as a side-income offer once it's separated from the unpaid context it was built in and named as the specific, marketable capability it actually is.

A note on skills you're still actively developing

Not every sellable skill needs to be fully mature before it clears the bar for a first side-income offer, and it's worth distinguishing this from the earlier warning against launching a skill with no real evidence behind it. A skill you've been developing seriously for six months to a year — real, deliberate practice, real feedback, visible improvement — can absolutely pass the four-step process in this chapter, provided the evidence you gather in Step 3 is honest about where you actually are. The difference between a legitimate, still-developing skill and one that isn't ready yet comes down to whether you can point to something concrete: a handful of completed pieces of work, a specific improvement you can demonstrate, feedback from people qualified to judge it.

If your evidence for a still-developing skill is thin, the honest move isn't to abandon the idea — it's to price accordingly, using an introductory rate at the very low end of your researched range from Chapter 3, and to be transparent with early clients about where you are in your development if directly asked, rather than overstating your experience. Plenty of real, sustainable side incomes started this way, with an early client getting a genuinely fair price in exchange for being part of the proof-building phase, and both sides knowing it. What doesn't work is skipping the evidence-gathering altogether and pricing a still-developing skill as though it already carried a full track record — that's a mismatch that tends to surface in the quality of the delivered work, not in the pricing conversation itself.

How this chapter's exercise differs from a general strengths assessment

It's worth distinguishing the four-step process in this chapter from the broader category of workplace strengths assessments and personality-based career tools many readers will have encountered before, since they can look superficially similar and produce very different results. A strengths assessment is typically built to describe a general disposition — someone who tests as a "connector" or an "analyzer" learns something true about how they tend to operate, but that description sits at a level of abstraction that, on its own, rarely produces a sellable offer without a great deal of additional translation work. The four-step process in this chapter is deliberately narrower and more concrete by design: it isn't asking what kind of person you are, it's asking what specific, provable outcome you can produce for someone else, backed by evidence you can point to today.

This distinction matters practically, not just conceptually. If you've taken a strengths assessment in the past and found the results interesting but never actionable, that's not a failure of self-knowledge — it's a mismatch between the tool's purpose and the specific, concrete task this chapter is built for. Feel free to let a broad self-description like "I'm naturally curious" or "I'm a connector" inform which raw-list items feel worth pursuing, but don't stop there — every item on the list still needs to survive the Stranger Test and the evidence check before it counts as a real answer to the question this chapter is actually asking.

Chapter 2 — Turning a Skill Into an Offer Someone Can Actually Buy

The mechanics of packaging, scoping, and naming a first deliverable

The situation

An HVAC technician spends his weekends helping neighbors and coworkers with small home repair jobs — a rattling ceiling fan here, a thermostat that won't hold a schedule there — and never charges more than gas money, because he doesn't think of it as a business, just a favor he happens to be equipped to do. When a coworker suggests he "should really charge for that," his honest response is: charge for what, exactly? There's no consistent list of what he does, no starting price, nothing a stranger could point to and say "yes, I want that." He has a skill. He doesn't have an offer.

The mechanics

A skill and an offer are not the same thing, and the gap between them is where most side-income attempts stall before they ever earn a dollar. A skill is a capability. An offer is that capability packaged into something specific enough for a stranger to say yes to without a lengthy back-and-forth first: a defined scope, a defined deliverable, and — critically — a name that describes the outcome rather than the process.

The naming part matters more than it seems like it should. "I fix small home stuff on weekends" is a skill description. "Weekend Home Tune-Up: a two-hour visit where I check and adjust your thermostat, tighten and rebalance ceiling fans, and flag anything bigger before it becomes an emergency repair" is an offer. The second version does three things the first doesn't: it tells the buyer exactly what they're getting, it tells them roughly how long it takes (which implies a price range before you even state one), and it frames the value in terms of what it prevents, not just what it does in the moment.

This packaging step is also what separates a real side income from an endless string of one-off favors. A favor gets negotiated fresh every single time, from scratch, with no shared reference point — which is exhausting for you and confusing for the buyer. A packaged offer gets referred. When someone says "you should talk to my technician friend," they need something specific to point the referral toward. “He’s good with home stuff” produces nothing. “He does a two-hour tune-up visit, it’s like eighty bucks, get on his list before winter” produces a client.

There’s a related mechanism worth understanding, too, because it explains why a specific offer converts even a stranger who’s never met you: a defined scope reduces the buyer’s perceived risk of saying yes. An open-ended “I help with home stuff” leaves the buyer to imagine every possible way the arrangement could go wrong or balloon in scope — how long will it take, what if it turns into something bigger, what happens if I’m not happy. A tightly scoped offer answers those unspoken questions before they’re even asked, which is a large part of why the exact same skill sells at a meaningfully higher rate once it’s properly packaged than it did as an informal favor, even before a single dollar of price negotiation happens. The packaging itself is doing real selling work, independent of the price attached to it.

The script and framework

Step 1 — Narrow the skill from Chapter 1 into a single, specific deliverable. Not "I help with home repairs" but one concrete thing: a specific visit, a specific document, a specific fixed piece of work with a clear start and end. If your skill naturally supports several different deliverables, pick one to start — the narrowest, clearest one — rather than launching with a menu. A menu is a Chapter 9 problem, once you have clients asking for more.

Step 2 — Define the scope in writing, even if it's only for yourself at first. What's included. What's explicitly not included. How long it takes. What the buyer needs to provide or prepare in advance. This isn't paperwork for its own sake — a scope written down before you ever talk to a buyer is what keeps a two-hour job from quietly becoming a four-hour job because nobody set a boundary out loud.

Step 3 — Name the offer around the outcome, not the activity. A useful test: if you read the name to someone with zero context, does it tell them what they'd walk away with? "Lesson Plan Builder" describes an activity. "One Week of Ready-to-Teach Biology Lessons, Built to Your District's

Standards” describes an outcome. The second version does more selling in its own title than a paragraph of description could do for the first.

Step 4 — Write a single paragraph you could send a real person today. Three sentences: what it is, what it includes, and roughly what it costs or how pricing works (full pricing mechanics come in Chapter 3 — for now, even a placeholder range is enough to make the offer feel real rather than hypothetical). This paragraph is your first real asset. You’ll reuse it, almost unchanged, in the outreach scripts in Chapter 4.

A template for that paragraph:

> “I put together [specific deliverable] for [specific type of buyer] — it includes [two or three concrete things], takes about [timeframe], and runs [price or price range]. If that’s useful, happy to talk through what you need.”

Treat the first version of this paragraph as a draft, not a finished asset — send it to two or three people you trust, before ever sending it to a real prospect, and ask them plainly whether it’s clear or confusing. A single round of that kind of feedback, gathered deliberately rather than skipped in the interest of moving fast, routinely catches a vague phrase or an unclear scope boundary that would otherwise cost you a first client's confidence before you'd even had a chance to demonstrate the work itself.

Worked example

The HVAC technician narrows down to a single deliverable: a two-hour "Weekend Home Tune-Up" — thermostat check and reprogram, ceiling fan balance and tighten on up to four fans, and a written list of anything bigger he noticed that's worth addressing before it becomes a real repair. He writes the scope out: included, not included (no actual repairs during the visit itself — those get quoted separately, keeping the tune-up fast and predictably priced), timeframe, what the homeowner needs to have ready (clear access to the thermostat and any fans, nothing else).

He names it "The Weekend Home Tune-Up" and writes his one-paragraph offer: "I do a two-hour home tune-up on weekends — thermostat check and reprogramming, up to four ceiling fans balanced and tightened, plus a written list of anything bigger I spot that's worth addressing before it turns into a real repair. Runs $95 flat. Happy to get you on the schedule if that's useful." He sends a version of this exact paragraph to four people who'd previously gotten the work for free, and two of them book immediately — not because the skill changed, but because there was finally something specific to say yes to.

A second worked example

A massage therapist who works full time at a physical therapy clinic wants to build a side offer around a specific technique she's developed for desk workers with chronic neck and shoulder tension. Her raw skill — "I'm good at massage" — is far too broad to sell on its own; everyone who does this work professionally could say the same thing. She narrows it down: a 45-minute session specifically targeting the upper back, neck, and forearms, aimed at people whose pain comes from long hours at a desk, paired with three simple stretches written out for the client to do between sessions.

She names it "The Desk Worker Reset" and writes her scope: what's included (the session itself, plus the written stretch sheet), what's not (this isn't a substitute for a referral to a physical therapist if something's genuinely wrong, and she says so plainly in her offer description), the timeframe, and what a client should wear. Her one-paragraph offer reads: "I run a 45-minute session built specifically for desk-related neck and shoulder tension — deep work on the upper back, neck, and forearms, plus three stretches you can do at your desk between sessions. $85, evenings and Saturdays. Happy to answer questions if that's useful." The specificity — desk workers, upper back and forearms, not a general relaxation massage — is what makes the offer memorable enough to refer, in a field where "I do massage" is a crowded, generic claim.

Frequently misunderstood point: a tighter offer isn't a smaller offer

A common hesitation at this stage is the sense that narrowing an offer down to one specific deliverable somehow shrinks the business, as though a wide menu of services signals more ambition than a single, well-defined one. The opposite is usually true in practice. A single, clearly packaged offer is what makes an early side income legible to a stranger and referable by an existing client — a menu of six loosely defined services is harder to explain, harder to price consistently, and harder for anyone to recommend, because "he does a bunch of different handyman stuff" doesn't give a referral anywhere specific to point. The narrow offer isn't a smaller ambition. It's the version of the business that's actually possible to sell before you have the reputation to sell a broader one.

Scoping tightly enough that "yes" is easy

A common mistake at this stage is building an offer so broad that saying yes to it feels like a bigger commitment than it needs to be. "I'll help with your home maintenance" asks a buyer to imagine an open-ended relationship. "A two-hour visit, flat price, here's exactly what's included" asks them to imagine a single Saturday morning. The second is a dramatically easier yes, and getting a first yes quickly matters more at this stage than capturing every dollar of value you could theoretically deliver. Broaden the offer later, once you have a client relationship and real trust to build on — Chapter 9 covers exactly that expansion. At the start, the tightest, clearest, easiest-to-say-yes-to version of the offer beats the most comprehensive one every time.

Common objections and how to handle them

"What if narrowing my offer means I'm turning away work I could otherwise get?" In the very short term, sometimes, yes — a narrow offer occasionally loses a buyer who wanted something slightly different from what you've packaged. But a narrow, specific offer converts a much higher percentage of the people it does reach, and it's dramatically easier to describe, refer, and price confidently. A broad, vague offer that converts poorly produces fewer total clients than a narrow one that converts well, even though the broad version theoretically covers more ground. Start narrow, and let real client requests — not your own guessing — tell you where to widen later.

"What if I don't know the exact timeframe or scope until I actually do the work once?" This is normal for a genuinely first-time offer, and the honest fix is to build your first scope estimate from your best guess, deliver it once, and revise the written scope immediately afterward based on what you actually learned. Treat your first one or two clients partly as a pricing and scoping pilot, not just a transaction — the goal is a scope description by client three that's grounded in real experience rather than a guess made before you'd ever done the work.

"What if my deliverable doesn't have a natural, catchy name?" A name doesn't need to be clever — it needs to be clear. "One Week of Ready-to-Teach Biology Lessons" isn't catchy in a marketing sense, but it's instantly understandable, which matters more at this stage than sounding polished. Resist the urge to spend real time searching for a clever brand name before you've sold the offer even once; a plain, descriptive name is a perfectly good starting point; you can always refine it once the offer has real traction.

A note on offers with recurring delivery versus a single deliverable

Some skills naturally support a one-time deliverable — a finished set of lesson plans, a single home tune-up visit, a completed resume. Others naturally support a recurring relationship — ongoing social media management, a monthly content retainer, a weekly dog-walking route. Both are legitimate starting offers, but they carry different scoping considerations worth deciding on up front rather than discovering mid-relationship. A recurring offer needs an explicit cadence (weekly, monthly), an explicit cancellation or pause policy, and a clear boundary on what happens if the buyer's needs change mid-cycle — none of which a one-time offer has to address at all. If your skill naturally supports both a one-time and a recurring version, it's usually easier to start with the one-time version, prove the offer works, and introduce a recurring version once you have real evidence of what ongoing delivery actually requires from you.

A full conversation, start to finish

It helps to see the offer paragraph from this chapter inside a real exchange, rather than only as an isolated message.

Neighbor: "Hey, I heard you're doing some handyman stuff now — what exactly do you do?"

Technician: "I do a two-hour home tune-up on weekends — thermostat check and reprogramming, up to four ceiling fans balanced and tightened, plus a written list of anything bigger I spot that's worth addressing before it turns into a real repair. Runs $95 flat."

Neighbor: "Oh, that's perfect actually — our thermostat's been acting up and one of the fans wobbles like it's going to fall off the ceiling."

Technician: "That's exactly the kind of thing this covers. I've got Saturday morning open this week if that works."

Neighbor: "That works great — do I need to do anything to get ready for it?"

Technician: "Just clear access to the thermostat and whichever fans you want looked at — that's it."

Notice how little explaining the offer requires once it's actually built correctly. The technician doesn't describe his general capabilities or list his years of experience — he states the packaged deliverable, answers the follow-up question with a specific detail rather than a vague reassurance, and the whole exchange moves from question to booked appointment in under a minute. That speed is the entire point of the packaging work in this chapter — an offer this specific removes almost all of the friction a vaguer description would have introduced.

A short exercise before you move to Chapter 3

Write your one-paragraph offer from Step 4, then read it out loud to someone who has no context on what you do — a partner, a friend, anyone willing to listen for thirty seconds. Ask them a single question afterward: "based on what I just said, what would you expect to get, and roughly what would you expect to pay?" If their answer matches what you actually intended, the offer is clear enough to send to a real prospect. If it doesn't match, the gap between what you meant and what they heard is exactly what needs tightening before Chapter 4.

Turning several related skills into a small family of offers, without diluting the first one

Some people finish Chapter 1 with more than one skill that clearly passes the Stranger Test, and the temptation is to build all of them into offers at once, on the theory that more offers means more chances to land a client. Resist this in the early going. A single, tightly packaged offer, launched and proven first, gives you a clean, referable story and a fast path to a first client, exactly as this chapter describes. Two or three offers launched simultaneously split your limited early hours across untested ideas at once, and they split a stranger's attention too — a person deciding whether to hire you is generally better served by one clear, specific option than by a menu to sort through before they've even decided whether they trust you.

The right time to add a second offer is after the first one has a real track record — completed projects, at least one strong testimonial, evidence of what actually sells and what doesn't. At that point, a second offer built from a related skill can genuinely complement the first rather than compete with it for attention. The pharmacy technician from Chapter 3, for instance, might eventually add a second offer — a short in-office training session on patient communication — once her patient-education-sheet business has enough of a track record to make the second offer credible on the strength of the first. Introduced too early, before either offer has proof behind it, the same expansion reads as unfocused rather than complementary, and it usually slows down the very first sale this chapter is built to produce.

When you do add a second offer, keep them visibly distinct rather than blurring them into a single vague description of "everything I do." A buyer should be able to tell, quickly, which specific offer solves their specific problem — the same clarity principle from Step 3's naming guidance, applied now across a small, deliberately built portfolio rather than a single deliverable.

Testing an offer before fully committing to it

For anyone hesitant to lock in a scope and a name before knowing whether the offer will actually resonate, it's worth building in a small, low-risk testing step before going all in. Describe the offer, in its full packaged form from this chapter, to three or four people who genuinely fit the target buyer profile but aren't part of your immediate circle — not to sell them anything yet, but specifically to ask whether the description makes sense and whether they'd realistically consider something like it. This is a smaller, more targeted version of the same feedback loop from this chapter's short exercise, aimed specifically at validating the offer's shape before it's ever priced or pitched for real.

Genuine, specific pushback at this stage — "I wouldn't know when I'd need that" or "that sounds like it's really for a bigger business than mine" — is valuable information worth acting on before Chapter 4's outreach begins, not a discouraging signal to push through. A small adjustment to scope or framing made now, based on real feedback from people who match your actual buyer, is far cheaper than discovering the same mismatch after several rounds of outreach have already gone out with a version of the offer that wasn't quite landing.

Offers that involve a physical product versus a service

Everything in this chapter's scoping guidance transfers cleanly to a service-based offer, but a physical-product offer — the machinist's custom signage, a handmade good, anything with real materials attached — carries one additional scoping decision worth addressing explicitly: what happens to materials cost if a client cancels or changes their mind partway through. A service offer generally has little sunk cost if a client backs out early, but a physical-product offer may already have committed real money to materials by the time a change happens.

The fix is a simple, stated policy decided in advance rather than negotiated awkwardly after the fact — a deposit sized to cover materials cost, taken before work begins, non-refundable if the client cancels after materials are purchased, clearly stated as part of the offer itself rather than buried in fine print discovered only when a cancellation actually happens. This single addition protects a physical-product side income from a specific risk a pure service offer doesn't carry, and it's a normal, expected term for this kind of work — most buyers of custom physical goods have encountered a deposit requirement before and won't find it unusual.

Chapter 3 — Pricing Your First Offer With No Track Record

Setting a number when you don't yet have proof anyone will pay it

The situation

A pharmacy technician wants to start doing freelance patient-education content for independent pharmacies and small clinics — short, clear handouts on medication timing, common side effects, and insurance basics, the kind of material most small practices know they need and never get around to writing well. She has the clinical knowledge and, it turns out, a real gift for making it readable. What she doesn't have is any idea what to charge. A search online produces numbers from twenty-five dollars to a thousand dollars for what sounds like the same kind of work, with no clear reason why. She picks a number that feels safely low, mostly because a low number feels less likely to get laughed out of the room — and immediately underprices herself in a way that will be hard to correct later.

The mechanics

Pricing a first offer is a genuinely different problem from pricing an established one, which is why it gets its own chapter here rather than deferring to general pricing theory. An established freelancer or business owner has a track record — past clients, results, testimonials — that lets a price be justified by evidence. A first-time offer has none of that. The entire pricing decision has to be made on cost, comparable market rates, and a clear-eyed view of what the first few sales are actually for, which isn't the same thing as maximizing revenue.

There are three legitimate ways to build a first price, and most people accidentally default to the worst of the three: guessing based on what feels comfortable to ask for, which is really just a measure of your own comfort with asking, not a measure of the work's value.

The first legitimate method is cost-plus: what does this cost you in time and materials, plus a margin. This is a useful floor, not a ceiling — it tells you the number below which you're effectively working for less than your time is worth, but it doesn't tell you what the market will actually bear.

The second is comparable-market pricing: what do people with similar (not identical, similar) skills charge for similar work, adjusted down slightly for the fact that you don't yet have a track record to point to. This is usually the most useful anchor for a first price, because it roots the number in something real rather than a guess.

The third, and the one that actually resolves the tension between the first two, is thinking clearly about what a first sale is for. A first client at a lower-than-ideal price who becomes a real testimonial and a source of referral is worth more, long-term, than a slightly higher price with no client at all. This isn't an argument for underpricing indefinitely — it's an argument for a deliberately time-limited introductory price, used to generate the proof a first-time offer doesn't yet have, with a clear, pre-decided point at which the price goes up regardless of how comfortable the lower number has become to charge.

It's worth understanding, too, why a first-time price feels so much harder to state than a price you've charged a hundred times before, because the discomfort itself is genuinely informative. Every previous chapter of pricing advice most people have absorbed, informally, tends to be built for someone with an established track record — charge what you're worth, know your value, don't undersell yourself — and all of it assumes evidence exists to anchor "worth" against. A genuinely first-time offer has no such evidence yet, which is exactly why generic pricing confidence advice tends to feel hollow at this specific stage: it's answering a question about conviction when the real, more solvable problem is a lack of information. The cost-plus floor and the comparable-market range in this chapter exist specifically to replace that missing evidence with real numbers, so the eventual price isn't a test of nerve — it's the output of a calculation.

The script and framework

Step 1 — Calculate your cost-plus floor. Estimate the real hours a deliverable takes, including the parts people forget to count — revisions, communication, any research or setup time. Multiply by a minimum hourly rate you'd genuinely accept for this kind of work, then add a margin of at least 20 to 30 percent to account for the hours that don't show up in a clean estimate. This is your floor. Don't price below it, even for a first client, because a price that doesn't clear your own real costs teaches you nothing except that side income is a bad use of your time — a false lesson caused by mispricing, not by the actual market.

Step 2 — Research three to five comparable prices. Not for an identical service — those are rare — but for genuinely comparable scope and skill level, from people who are further along than you but not wildly more established. Freelance marketplaces, professional communities in your field, and direct conversations with people doing adjacent work are all legitimate sources. You're building a range, not a single number.

Step 3 — Set an introductory price at the low end of your researched range, but never below your cost-plus floor. This is the number for your first three to five clients, explicitly framed to yourself (not necessarily to the client) as an introductory rate you're using to build proof, not your permanent price.

Step 4 — Decide your graduation trigger in advance, before you have any clients at all. Pick a specific, concrete trigger that moves you off the introductory price and onto a standard one — a number of completed projects (three to five is typical), a specific testimonial or result in hand, or a calendar date, whichever fits your situation. Write it down. The single most common pricing mistake at this stage isn't setting an introductory price — it's never leaving it, because there's no natural moment that forces the conversation, and a below-market number quietly becomes the permanent number by default.

A script for stating a first-time price with appropriate confidence, without over-explaining an introductory rate you don't owe anyone an apology for:

> “For [the specific deliverable], I'm at $[introductory price] right now. That includes [what's included]. I can walk you through the details if that's helpful.”

Step 5 — Write your graduation trigger somewhere you'll actually see it, and treat crossing it as a scheduled event, not an emotional decision. A calendar reminder, a note pinned to the top of a tracking spreadsheet, a specific line in the same document where you're logging clients — the format matters less than the fact that it's external to your own memory. A trigger that exists only as an intention in your head is the version of this step that quietly never gets acted on, which is exactly how an introductory price becomes a permanent one without anyone deciding that outcome on purpose.

Worked example

The pharmacy technician calculates her cost-plus floor: roughly three hours per practice's initial set of education sheets, at a personal minimum of $35 an hour, plus a 25 percent margin, landing her floor at $131. She researches comparable freelance health-content work and finds a credible range of $150 to $400 for a similar-scoped initial project, with most first-time providers in adjacent fields landing near the bottom of that range.

She sets her introductory price at $175 — above her floor, near the low end of her researched range — and decides in advance that her graduation trigger is three completed projects or ninety days, whichever comes first. She lands her first practice at $175, uses the finished materials and the practice owner's enthusiastic feedback as her first piece of real proof, and by her fourth practice — past her own graduation trigger — she raises the standard price to $275, using the same evidence-based confidence from the earlier chapters of this series to hold the new number without apologizing for the increase.

A second worked example

A machinist who spends weekends building custom metal signage — shop signs, house numbers, decorative pieces — wants to start selling the work rather than giving it away to friends who admire it. His cost-plus floor is more complex than a service-based offer, since it has to account for material cost as well as time: roughly $40 in raw steel and consumables for a typical mid-sized sign, four hours of his own time at a $30 personal minimum, plus a 30 percent margin to cover the wear on his equipment and the inevitable piece that doesn't come out right on the first attempt. His floor lands at $234.

He researches comparable custom metalwork online and through a local maker community and finds a real range of $250 to $600 for similar-scoped signage, depending heavily on size and design complexity. He sets his introductory price at $265 for a standard-sized sign, just above his floor and at the low end of his researched range, and sets his graduation trigger at five completed pieces — a slightly higher number than the pharmacy technician's, because he wants a broader sample of different design requests before locking in a standard price across a genuinely variable kind of work. By his sixth piece, he raises his standard price to $340 and introduces a separate, higher tier for larger or more complex custom designs, priced individually rather than at a single flat rate — a structural change in his pricing that the introductory period's real data made possible in a way a guess at the outset never could have.

The trap of pricing to avoid rejection

It helps to say directly what actually drives most first-time underpricing, because it isn't really about the market — it's about wanting a "yes" badly enough to set a number that feels impossible to refuse. This produces exactly the outcome it's trying to avoid: a client who says yes instantly to a suspiciously low price is sometimes a great client and sometimes a signal that the number was set too low to filter for anyone who takes the work seriously. A price set at your genuine floor, researched against a real comparable range, filters naturally for buyers who value the work appropriately — and a "no" from someone who wasn't going to be a good client anyway costs you nothing you actually needed.

A full pricing conversation, start to finish

It helps to see the introductory-price script from earlier in this chapter inside a real exchange, rather than only as an isolated line.

Prospective client: "So what would something like this run?"

Technician: "For a full set of patient-education sheets covering your most common medications, I'm at $175 right now. That includes four sheets, one round of revisions, and a plain-language pass so they read well for an actual patient, not just clinically. I can walk you through exactly what's covered if that's helpful."

Prospective client: "That's very reasonable — can we start with two sheets first, just to see how it goes?"

Technician: "Sure — for two sheets specifically, I'd do that at $110, and if you want the full set of four afterward, I'll apply the difference toward the full price."

Notice what the technician does in the second reply: she doesn't just shrink her price proportionally by guessing — she has a specific, pre-considered number ready for a smaller scope, because she'd thought through the likely variations on her offer before the conversation happened, not during it. That preparation is what keeps a scope-reduction request from turning into an improvised discount.

Adapting pricing across different offer types

The cost-plus-and-comparable-range method in this chapter applies most directly to project-based or session-based offers, but the framework shifts a little for other common offer structures. For recurring, subscription-style offers — a monthly retainer, a weekly service — price per cycle rather than trying to back into an hourly-equivalent number, since buyers evaluate a recurring price against the value of the whole cycle, not against an hourly rate they're unlikely to calculate themselves. For offers where the deliverable's scope varies significantly client to client — custom furniture, bespoke design work — a stated starting price ("starting at $X, final quote depends on scope") does more work than a single fixed number, because it sets a credible floor without promising a number you can't actually honor once you see the real scope. For skill-based hourly work where scope genuinely can't be estimated in advance, an hourly rate with a not-to-exceed estimate for the first engagement gives a first-time client the predictability they need without forcing you to guess at a fixed project price you might regret.

Frequently misunderstood point: an introductory price isn't the same as a permanent discount

It's easy to conflate the introductory pricing strategy in this chapter with a general instinct to keep prices low as a way of staying competitive indefinitely — but the two are structurally different, and the difference matters. An introductory price is a deliberate, time-limited tool used specifically to generate proof a first-time offer doesn't yet have, with a graduation trigger decided before the first client is ever found. A permanent low price, by contrast, isn't a strategy at all — it's a default that never got revisited, and it caps what the offer can earn indefinitely regardless of how much real proof accumulates behind it. The entire value of Step 4's graduation trigger is that it forces the distinction: without a specific, written trigger, an introductory price and a permanent underpricing habit are functionally identical, and only one of them was ever supposed to be permanent.

A short exercise before you move to Chapter 4

Write down your cost-plus floor and your researched comparable range side by side, then write your introductory price and your graduation trigger underneath both. Put a specific date on your calendar — ninety days out, or whatever fits your graduation trigger — labeled clearly as your pricing check-in. When that date arrives, look at how many projects you've actually completed against your trigger and raise your price then, on schedule, rather than waiting for a moment that feels emotionally right, which for most people never quite arrives on its own.

Pricing when the cost of each project genuinely varies

Some offers have a fairly consistent, predictable cost from client to client, which is what makes a flat introductory price workable. Others — the machinist's custom signage from earlier in this chapter, a caterer's per-event costs, a seamstress's material-heavy alterations — have real, meaningful cost variance built into the work itself, where one project might cost twice as much in materials or time as another that looks superficially similar on the surface. Applying a single flat introductory price across genuinely variable-cost work risks either badly underpricing the expensive projects or badly overpricing the cheap ones, neither of which serves the pricing research this chapter is built around.

The fix is to separate the pricing decision into two layers rather than one. First, build a base introductory price for a clearly defined "standard" version of the offer — a specific, typical scope you can describe precisely, the way the machinist defined a standard-sized sign. Second, build a simple, transparent adjustment rule for scope that falls outside the standard — a stated per-square-foot rate for a larger sign, a stated additional charge for a design with meaningfully more complexity, a clear formula rather than a case-by-case guess each time. This keeps the introductory-pricing discipline from this chapter intact — a real floor, a real researched range, a real graduation trigger — while still accounting honestly for the cost variance that a single flat number can't absorb without either shortchanging you or over-charging a client whose project genuinely required less.

Write the adjustment rule down before your first client, the same way you write down the base introductory price — a rule decided in advance, calmly, is far easier to apply consistently and explain to a client than one improvised in the moment a larger-than-typical request arrives.

What to do if a prospect asks your rate before you've finished researching it

Sometimes a real prospect appears before the research step in this chapter is fully complete — an unexpected inquiry, an eager referral, a conversation that moves faster than planned. The instinct in the moment is often to give a rushed, unresearched number just to keep the conversation moving, which is exactly the guessing trap this chapter opens by warning against. A better response, and one that costs you nothing in credibility, is a short, honest delay: "I want to give you an accurate number rather than a rough guess — can I follow up by tomorrow with a firm price?" This is a completely normal request in any professional context, and it buys the exact time needed to finish the cost-plus calculation and the comparable-market research properly, rather than anchoring your entire pricing structure to a number invented under pressure in a single conversation.

The only version of this to avoid is silence without a stated reason — simply not responding for several days with no explanation reads very differently than a specific, professional request for a short, named delay. The difference between the two is a single sentence, and it's worth having that sentence ready before you ever need it.

Raising the introductory price mid-batch, honestly

Occasionally the graduation trigger from Step 4 arrives in the middle of an active project or an already-agreed engagement with a client still working under the introductory price. The right approach is straightforward and worth deciding in advance rather than improvising in the moment: honor the introductory price for any client who agreed to it before the trigger was hit, in full, for the entire scope they signed up for — raising a price mid-engagement on someone who committed under a different number, even if your own internal trigger has since been crossed, damages trust in a way that's disproportionate to the money involved. The new, standard price applies cleanly to every new client going forward, starting from the graduation date, with no ambiguity about which price applies to whom.

This distinction is worth stating plainly to yourself in writing at the moment you cross the trigger — a short note listing exactly which existing clients remain at the introductory rate through the end of their current engagement, and confirming that every new inquiry from that date forward gets quoted at the new, standard number. A little bit of administrative clarity at this transition point prevents both the discomfort of accidentally underpricing a new client out of habit and the far worse mistake of appearing to renegotiate a price with someone who already agreed to a different one in good faith.

Chapter 4 — Getting Your First Client Without a Marketing Budget

The actual channels and the actual words, ranked by how well they convert

The situation

A warehouse forklift operator has spent two years building custom furniture on weekends — a hobby that started with a single bookshelf and grew into a small collection of finished pieces sitting in his garage, each one better than the last. He has, by any reasonable standard, an offer: he's good, he's improving fast, and the work photographs well. What he doesn't have is a single client, because every time he considers how to find one, his mental image is a business he doesn't have — a website, an ad budget, a following — none of which he can build in the time or money he actually has available. He's stuck not because the offer is weak, but because he's aiming at the wrong first channel entirely.

The mechanics

There's a strict hierarchy of how likely different outreach channels are to produce a first client, and it runs almost exactly backward from where most first-timers instinctively start. Cold, public channels — a new website, a social media account with no following, a marketplace listing among thousands of others — have the lowest conversion rate for a first sale, because they require a stranger to evaluate you with zero trust signal beyond what you've written about yourself. Warm channels — people who already know you, or people one degree removed through someone who knows you — convert dramatically better, because trust is already partially established before the conversation even starts.

This isn't a permanent state of affairs. Cold channels become genuinely useful once you have real proof — finished work, a testimonial, a specific result — because that proof does the trust-building job a stranger's website visit can't do on its own. But at the very start, before any of that proof exists, warm channels aren't just easier, they're structurally more likely to work at all, which is why this chapter puts them first regardless of how much less exciting they sound than "build an audience."

The specific mechanism behind why warm outreach converts so much better than cold outreach is worth understanding directly: a request from someone you already know activates social proof and reciprocity at the same time — the listener already has a baseline of trust in you as a person, and there's frequently an implicit sense of goodwill (a favor owed, a friendship, a shared history) that lowers the bar for saying yes to a first, small ask. Cold outreach has neither of those things working in its favor, which is exactly why it requires either a much larger volume of attempts or much stronger existing proof to convert at a similar rate.

This is also why "build an audience first" is such common but frequently misapplied advice for a first-time side income. Building a public following is a genuinely useful long-term channel, and it eventually becomes a real asset — but it's slow, it requires consistent effort with no guaranteed payoff, and it asks a genuinely new offer to convert cold strangers before it has any of the proof that makes cold conversion realistic in the first place. The warm-list approach in this chapter isn't a lesser substitute for audience-building; it's the correct sequence —

proof first, through people who already trust you, and a public audience later, once that proof exists to make the cold version of the pitch actually land.

The script and framework

Step 1 — Build a warm list of fifteen to twenty-five names before doing anything else. Not close friends specifically, and not a random contact dump — people who might plausibly need what you're offering, or who know someone who might. Coworkers, former coworkers, neighbors, people from any community you're part of, family members with their own networks. Write the list down; don't try to hold it in your head.

Step 2 — Send a specific, low-pressure message to the warm list, not a vague announcement. The mistake most people make here is posting a single generic "starting a side business, let me know if you're interested!" update and treating that as having covered the warm-outreach step. It doesn't work nearly as well as a specific, individually sent message, because a generic post asks the reader to imagine their own use case unprompted, while a specific message does that imagining for them.

A script for warm outreach:

> “Hey [name] — random thought, but I’ve started [doing the specific offer] on the side. I did [specific proof point, even a small one] and it went really well. If you or anyone you know could use [specific outcome], I’d love to help — no pressure either way.”

Step 3 — Ask every warm contact for a referral, whether or not they need the offer themselves. This single question — “do you know anyone who might need this?” — is the highest-leverage sentence in early-stage outreach, and it’s the one most people forget to include. Most of your warm list won’t personally need your specific offer. Many of them know someone who does.

Step 4 — Once the warm list is exhausted, move to narrow, targeted cold outreach rather than broad public posting. A targeted cold message to a specific person, referencing something specific about their situation, converts far better than a broad public post asking the internet in general. If you're a woodworker, a targeted message to a small local business whose furniture is visibly worn will convert better than a general post to a hobbyist forum, because it names a specific, visible problem rather than making a stranger do the work of imagining one.

Step 5 — Treat every completed first job as an asset, not just income. Photograph it, ask for a short, specific testimonial while the buyer's enthusiasm is fresh, and ask directly whether they'd be comfortable being referenced or referred. This is what converts your second and third clients from warm-list luck into a repeatable process — proof, used deliberately, is what eventually makes the cold channels from Step 4 start working at a normal rate instead of a slow one.

Keep a running log of everyone you've reached out to, their response, and any referral they've given, however small — a simple spreadsheet is enough. Without it, it's easy to lose track of who's already been asked, who owes you a follow-up, and who mentioned a referral in passing that never got a proper thank-you or check-in. This log becomes the backbone of your entire early client-acquisition effort, and it's the single tool most first-timers skip because it feels like unnecessary overhead at a stage when the whole list still fits in memory — right up until it doesn't.

Worked example

The furniture builder writes his warm list: nineteen names, including two former coworkers who'd complimented a piece on social media months earlier, a neighbor who'd mentioned needing a bench for her entryway, and several people from a community softball league he plays in. He sends individualized versions of the warm script to all nineteen over the course of a week, rather than one public post. Four people respond with genuine interest of their own. Six more, who don't need furniture themselves, offer a referral when asked directly — a question he'd never thought to include in previous, more passive attempts to "put the word out."

His neighbor books the entryway bench at his introductory price. He photographs the finished piece properly, in good light, and asks for a two-sentence testimonial once she's had it in her home for a week — she mentions specifically how well it fits the space, which becomes a real, usable line in his eventual outreach to strangers. Two of the six referrals turn into real conversations, one of which becomes his second paying client. None of this required a website, an ad, or a single stranger finding him by accident — it required a list, a specific message, and one added question most first-timers skip.

A second worked example

A wedding officiant, newly certified and looking to build a small side income around weekend ceremonies, has no warm list in the traditional sense — she doesn't personally know engaged couples in any meaningful number. Rather than treating this as a dead end for the warm-outreach approach, she widens the definition of "warm" to fit her actual situation: people who work adjacent to weddings and regularly get asked for vendor recommendations — a wedding photographer she knows socially, a florist from her neighborhood, the manager of a local event venue she's visited as a guest. None of them are potential clients themselves, but each one is regularly in a position to make exactly the kind of referral she needs.

She sends each of them a version of the warm script, adapted for a referral partner rather than a direct buyer: "Hey — wanted to let you know I'm now doing wedding officiant work on the side. I did a ceremony for [specific couple] last month and it went really well. If you ever have a couple looking for an officiant, I'd love an introduction — happy to send over more details if useful." Two of the three respond with genuine interest in referring her going forward, and the venue manager, in particular, adds her to a list of recommended vendors she hands new couples during their first tour — a single relationship that produces more consistent lead flow over the following year than any amount of cold outreach to engaged couples directly would have.

Common objections and how to handle them

"Isn't it awkward to ask people I know for business?" It can feel that way the first time, mostly because the request is unfamiliar rather than because it's actually imposing. The warm-outreach script in this chapter is built specifically to lower that discomfort — it names a specific offer, states real proof, and explicitly says "no pressure either way," which gives the recipient an easy, guilt-free out if they're not interested. Most people, asked this way, don't experience it as an imposition at all; they experience it as being let in on something the sender is proud of, which is a genuinely different feeling than being sold to.

"What if my warm list is small — fifteen or twenty people feels like nothing?" A small list still works, because the goal of Step 1 isn't to reach fifteen buyers directly — it's to reach fifteen people who might each know several more, through the referral question in Step 3. A list of fifteen honestly asked, each with their own separate network, routinely produces more real leads than a much larger list of strangers reached through a cold, generic post, because the conversion rate per contact is so much higher.

"What happens once the warm list and its referrals are exhausted?" This is exactly the moment Step 4's targeted cold outreach exists for, and by that point you're no longer approaching it with zero proof — you have at least one, ideally several, completed jobs, photographs, and a specific testimonial to draw on. Cold outreach done with real proof in hand converts meaningfully better than cold outreach attempted at the very start, which is part of why this chapter puts warm outreach first even for people who feel more comfortable with the anonymity of a cold, public post.

Frequently misunderstood point: referral partners aren’t the same as clients

A common oversight in early outreach is treating every contact as either a buyer or a dead end, which misses an entire category the wedding officiant’s example above depends on: people who will never buy the offer themselves but are structurally positioned to send buyers your way. A referral partner is worth cultivating with the same deliberateness as a client — a specific, individual message, a clear statement of what you do, and an explicit, direct ask for what you want from them, which in this case is an introduction rather than a purchase. Skipping this category because “they’re not a customer” leaves a genuinely high-leverage channel untouched, particularly for offers where the actual buyer is hard to reach directly but regularly passes through someone else’s orbit first.

A note on online marketplaces as a secondary channel

Freelance and service marketplaces — general platforms, or ones specific to a particular trade — can become a genuinely useful channel once an offer has real proof behind it, but they're a poor first channel for exactly the reason this chapter opens with: a stranger evaluating an unproven listing among hundreds of competing ones has no trust signal to work from beyond whatever you've written about yourself. Treat a marketplace listing as a Step 4 tool, built and populated with the photographs and testimonials generated by your warm-list clients, rather than as a Step 1 starting point. A listing built around real proof converts at a meaningfully different rate than the same listing built around promise alone.

A full conversation, start to finish

The warm-outreach script from earlier in this chapter, in a real exchange rather than as an isolated message.

Text message to a former coworker: "Hey! Random thought, but I've started building custom furniture on the side. Made a bookshelf and a bench recently that turned out really well — attaching a photo. If you or anyone you know could use a custom piece, I'd love to help. No pressure either way."

Reply: "Wait, this is beautiful, I had no idea you did this. We don't need anything right now but my sister just moved and mentioned wanting something for her hallway — want me to pass your info along?"

Text message: "That would be great, thank you! Whatever's easiest — happy to send more photos if that helps."

[Three days later]

Reply: "She just texted me, said she'll reach out this weekend."

Notice that the actual sale in this exchange doesn't happen in the conversation at all — it happens a week later, with someone the furniture builder has never spoken to directly, because the referral question did the work the original message alone couldn't have. This is the shape most warm outreach actually takes: not an instant transaction, but a short, low-pressure message that opens a door somewhere the sender couldn't have reached on their own.

A short exercise before you move to Chapter 5

Write your warm list of fifteen to twenty-five names right now, today, before reading further. Next to each name, write one honest sentence: what they might need themselves, or who they might know who does. Send the warm-outreach script to the first five names on the list within the next forty-eight hours. Momentum at this stage comes from a specific, time-bound first action, not from a plan to "start reaching out soon" — the plan without the deadline is exactly what kept the furniture builder in this chapter's opening scenario stuck for two years.

When interest doesn't turn into bookings

Sometimes the warm-outreach process in this chapter generates real, genuine interest — replies, questions, enthusiasm — that doesn't actually convert into a booked first client, and it's worth diagnosing why rather than concluding the whole approach isn't working. Three common causes are worth checking, in order. First, an unclear next step: interest that isn't met with a specific, easy action to take next — a suggested date, a direct link, a plain "want me to just go ahead and book this?" — often quietly fades, not because the interest wasn't real, but because the path from interest to commitment wasn't made obvious enough. Second, a price stated too vaguely or too late in the conversation, leaving the interested person unsure what they're actually agreeing to before they're asked to commit — revisit Chapter 3's discipline about stating a specific number plainly rather than leaving it open-ended. Third, and most common: the interest genuinely was polite rather than real, which happens more often with warm contacts than people expect, since a warm relationship makes it easy to express friendly enthusiasm without meaning to follow through.

The fix for the first two causes is mechanical — tighten the offer statement and add a specific, easy next step to every message going forward. The fix for the third is simply persistence and volume: not every warm contact converts, and a warm list of fifteen to twenty-five names is sized specifically to produce a handful of real bookings even accounting for a meaningful share of polite-but-not-genuine interest along the way.

Following up without being pushy

A single message, however well written, rarely captures every warm contact who might actually convert — people get busy, messages get buried, and a real yes sometimes just needs a gentle second nudge rather than being lost entirely. A single, well-timed follow-up, roughly a week after the original message, is a normal and expected part of outreach, not an imposition. Keep it short and low-pressure, referencing the original message rather than repeating the full pitch: "Just following up in case this got buried — totally fine if the timing isn't right, just wanted to check back." This respects the recipient's time while still giving a genuinely interested but distracted contact a clear second opportunity to respond.

One follow-up is standard practice. A second, unprompted follow-up after silence following the first one crosses into a different territory and is where the pushy feeling most people are worried about actually starts to show up — at that point, the more useful move is to let the specific contact go for now and focus your energy on the rest of the list, rather than continuing to press on a lead that's already had two clear opportunities to respond.

Reaching back out to a "not right now"

A contact who responds with genuine but not immediate interest — "this isn't the right time, but check back in a few months" — is a different case from silence, and deserves a different response than either a single follow-up or letting the lead go entirely. Note the specific timeframe they gave you, set an actual reminder for it, and reach back out when it arrives with a short, specific message referencing the original conversation: "You mentioned checking back around now — still interested in [the specific offer]?" This costs almost nothing and regularly converts contacts who were genuinely telling the truth about their timing rather than delivering a polite no in disguise. The distinction between the two isn't always obvious in the moment, which is exactly why it's worth taking a specific, timed "not right now" at face value and following up when they said to, rather than assuming it was a soft rejection and letting the opportunity quietly disappear.

Chapter 5 — Time-Boxing a Side Business Against a Full-Time Job

Protecting the job you need while building the thing that might replace it

The situation

A medical biller with a demanding full-time job starts taking on freelance virtual-assistant work for two small local businesses in the evenings. For the first month, it goes well — the extra income is real and immediate, and she likes the work. By month three, she's answering client messages during her lunch break at her actual job, staying up past midnight finishing deliverables, and starting to make small mistakes at work that never happened before. Nothing about the side income itself was the problem. The absence of any boundary between it and her actual job was.

The mechanics

A side income competes for exactly two finite resources: hours and attention, and it's the second one that gets underestimated far more often than the first. Most people planning a side income do a reasonably honest accounting of the hours — "I have Tuesday and Thursday evenings and part of Saturday" — and then fail to account for the fact that attention doesn't respect the boundaries hours are supposed to create. A side-income client message that arrives during a primary-job meeting pulls attention away from that meeting even if you don't respond to it until later, because now some part of your working memory is holding it.

This is the core mechanical risk this chapter addresses: a side income that isn't time-boxed doesn't stay contained to its allotted hours. It bleeds. And the direction it bleeds in matters, because the primary job is very often the thing funding the ability to take risks with the side income in the first place — health insurance, a stable paycheck, the runway that makes a slow first year of side income survivable rather than desperate. Protecting the primary job isn't caution for its own sake; it's protecting the actual foundation the side income depends on while it's still small.

The fix isn't discipline in the abstract sense — "just be more focused" — it's structural: specific blocks of time, specific rules about what happens outside those blocks, and specific communication with clients that sets expectations before a boundary gets tested rather than after it's already been crossed.

There's a second, quieter mechanical risk sitting alongside the attention problem: a side income without a stated boundary trains the people around it, gradually and without anyone intending it, to expect unlimited access. The medical biller's earlier clients didn't set out to demand lunch-break responses — they simply received them consistently enough that the pattern became an unstated norm, one that would have required an awkward, after-the-fact correction rather than a clean, upfront standard. Every unboundaried response sets a small precedent, and precedents accumulate quietly until an entire side income runs on an expectation nobody ever actually agreed to. Setting the standard in Step 2 before it's tested isn't just about the first message — it's about the entire shape of the relationship every message after it will follow.

The script and framework

Step 1 — Block specific, recurring hours for the side income, and treat them as fixed rather than flexible. Not "I'll work on it when I have time," which in practice means it gets the leftover hours after everything else, including rest, has already claimed its share. A specific block — Tuesday and Thursday, 7 to 9 p.m., and three hours on Saturday morning, for example — creates a container the work has to fit inside, rather than a container that expands to whatever the work demands.

Step 2 — Set and communicate a response-time standard to clients from the start, and hold it. Most side-income clients don't actually need an instant response; they need to know when to expect one. Stating this up front — "I typically respond within one business day" — does more to protect your attention during your primary job's hours than any amount of willpower, because it resets the client's expectation before urgency has a chance to build on their end.

Step 3 — Build a hard ceiling on total weekly side-income hours, and treat hitting it as a stop signal, not a suggestion. Decide the number in advance, based on an honest accounting of what your primary job and your own health can actually absorb without erosion — for most people starting out, somewhere between five and ten hours a week is a sustainable range, though the right number depends entirely on your specific job and life. When you hit the ceiling in a given week, the answer is to push non-urgent work to the following week, not to quietly extend the ceiling because a client asked nicely.

Step 4 — Separate the tools. A different email address, a different phone number if that's practical, a different calendar. This isn't about secrecy — it's about making the boundary visible to yourself, so that checking a side-income inbox during primary-job hours requires a deliberate action rather than happening automatically because it's the same inbox you're already staring at.

Step 5 — Build in a specific, recurring check on whether the primary job is showing strain. Once a month, honestly assess: has anything about your performance, energy, or attention at your primary job measurably slipped since starting the side income? If yes, the fix isn't guilt — it's reducing the side-income ceiling from Step 3 until the strain resolves, even if that means slower growth. A side income that costs you the job funding your health insurance and your runway isn't a net gain, no matter how well it's performing on its own terms.

These five steps work together as a system, not as a menu to pick from selectively — a blocked schedule without a stated response standard still leaves attention leaking outside the block, since clients with no stated expectation will simply message whenever, and a stated response standard without a hard hour ceiling still allows total volume to creep upward indefinitely even if individual response times stay disciplined. Put in place together, the five reinforce each other: the block defines when work happens, the standard manages expectations around it, the ceiling caps total volume, the separated tools make the boundary visible day to day, and the monthly check makes sure the whole system is actually holding rather than quietly eroding.

Worked example

The medical biller sets a firm block: Tuesday and Thursday, 7 to 9:30 p.m., and Saturday morning from 8 to 11. She creates a separate email address exclusively for the virtual-assistant work and removes it from her phone's notification settings, checking it only during her blocked hours and once briefly each morning before her actual job starts. She messages both existing clients with a simple, professional update: “Just a heads-up on how I manage response times — I typically get back to messages within one business day, usually faster, during my normal working hours for this. For anything urgent, flag it as urgent in the subject line and I’ll prioritize it.”

Neither client pushes back — in practice, neither had actually needed the near-instant responses she’d been providing during her lunch breaks; they’d simply gotten them because she was available, and availability quietly became an unstated expectation. She sets her weekly ceiling at eight hours and tracks it loosely in a notes app. In month four, she notices she’s approaching the ceiling two weeks in a row because a new client’s onboarding is heavier than usual — rather than absorbing it silently, she tells the new client honestly that full onboarding will take an extra week to stay within her existing commitments, and the client accepts it without friction. Her primary job’s performance, which had started slipping in the ungoverned version of this same arrangement, returns to normal within a month of the new structure.

A second worked example

A firefighter working a rotating schedule of 24-hour shifts followed by 48 hours off wants to build a side income coaching meal-prep for shift workers — a specific, well-evidenced skill drawn from years of feeding a full firehouse crew on a tight budget and tighter schedule. His challenge with time-boxing looks different from the medical biller's: he doesn't have a stable Tuesday-Thursday-evening kind of week to block against, because his own schedule shifts constantly.

He adapts Step 1 for his situation by setting a fixed weekly hour total — six hours — rather than fixed days, and decides at the start of each rotation which of his off days will hold those hours, based on his actual schedule that specific week. He sets his response standard slightly looser than a typical nine-to-five side income would need, given his own unusual hours: "I respond within two business days, since my own schedule rotates — for anything time-sensitive, text me directly." His hour ceiling stays fixed at six hours regardless of which specific days absorb it, and his monthly check-in focuses less on whether a fixed block held — it structurally can't, given his job — and more on whether the total hours crept upward past six in any given week, which is the actual signal that matters for someone with a genuinely irregular primary-job schedule.

When the ceiling and the opportunity conflict

Sometimes real opportunity arrives at a moment when your hour ceiling says no — a client offering significantly more work than you currently have capacity for, at a moment that happens to be genuinely good timing in every other respect. The instinct is almost always to say yes and figure out the hours later. Resist that instinct as a default. The honest options are: turn some of it down explicitly, negotiate a longer timeline that fits inside your existing ceiling rather than compressing the same amount of work into the same hours, or make a deliberate, time-limited exception with a clear end date and a clear plan to return to the normal ceiling afterward. What doesn't work, reliably, is treating every large opportunity as an unlimited exception, because that's exactly the pattern that turned the biller's first three months into the unsustainable version of this story.

Common objections and how to handle them

"What if my primary job's schedule is unpredictable and I can't commit to a fixed block?" Some jobs genuinely don't allow a fixed weekly block — rotating shifts, unpredictable overtime, on-call arrangements. In that case, replace the fixed-day version of Step 1 with a fixed-total: a specific number of hours per week, allocated to whatever days your actual schedule allows once it's known, decided at the start of each week rather than left open-ended day to day. The exact mechanism matters less than the discipline behind it — a known, bounded weekly total, chosen deliberately rather than absorbed passively into whatever hours happen to be left over.

"What if a client genuinely needs a faster response than my stated standard?" A stated response-time standard isn't a promise never to respond faster when something is truly urgent — it's a default that protects your attention during normal circumstances. Build a simple, explicit exception into the standard itself, as the biller did in her worked example, so a genuine emergency has a clear path to your attention without every message being treated as one.

"Won't clients think I'm not serious about the business if I'm not always available?" The opposite is usually true. A clear, professionally stated response standard reads as organized and established, not as uncommitted — freelancers and small businesses of every size operate this way, and clients accustomed to working with any professional service recognize a stated response window as normal practice rather than a red flag.

Frequently misunderstood point: the ceiling protects the business too, not just the job

Most of this chapter's framing centers on protecting the primary job from the side income's demands, which is the more urgent risk for most people starting out. But the hour ceiling and the time-blocking structure protect the side business in the other direction as well, in a way that's easy to overlook. Work delivered inside a rushed, boundary-free schedule — squeezed into lunch breaks, finished at midnight under fatigue — tends to be lower quality than the same work delivered inside a protected, planned block, and lower-quality delivery is exactly what erodes the referrals and repeat clients a young side income depends on most. The ceiling isn't only a defense of your primary job's performance. It's also a defense of the side income's own reputation, which suffers just as much from an exhausted, rushed version of the work as your day job does.

A note on protecting the relationship with your primary employer

Beyond the practical time-management concerns in this chapter, it's worth thinking specifically about how your side income interacts with your employer relationship itself. Check your employment agreement, if one exists, for any clause addressing outside work, conflicts of interest, or moonlighting — most such clauses are aimed at direct competitors or uses of employer resources, not at an unrelated side income run on your own time and equipment, but it's worth knowing what your specific agreement actually says rather than assuming. If your side income is in any way adjacent to your employer's business, a brief, honest conversation with a manager about what you're doing on your own time, framed plainly and without over-explaining, is usually a smaller risk than being asked about it later and having it look like something you were hiding.

Warning signs the boundary is already slipping

A few concrete signals worth checking against your own week, since they tend to appear gradually and are easy to rationalize individually even though the pattern together is unmistakable. You've responded to a side-income message during a primary-job meeting or task more than once in the past two weeks. You've stayed up meaningfully later than planned to finish side-income work more than once in the past month. A specific task or deadline at your primary job has slipped, even slightly, since starting the side income, and you've noticed but haven't addressed it. You've stopped checking your side-income hours against your stated ceiling because tracking it has started to feel like an unwelcome chore rather than a helpful habit. Any single one of these, on its own, might be a one-off. Two or more showing up together in the same month is the moment to apply Step 5's monthly check-in immediately, rather than waiting for the scheduled date.

A short exercise before you move to Chapter 6

Write down your specific weekly time block, your response-time standard, and your hour ceiling, all three, in one place — your calendar, a notes app, wherever you'll actually see it again. Then write the single monthly check-in question from Step 5 as a recurring calendar reminder, dated one month out. The structure in this chapter only works if it's revisited on a schedule; written down once and never checked again, it decays back into the same ungoverned pattern the biller started with.

Time-boxing when household responsibilities are shared

Everything in this chapter assumes the hours in question are fully yours to allocate, but for anyone sharing a household with a partner, roommate, or co-parent, a side income's hour block also draws against shared time and shared responsibilities in a way that's worth addressing directly rather than assuming it'll sort itself out. A weekly block that quietly shifts childcare, chores, or other shared obligations onto someone else, without an explicit conversation, tends to produce quiet resentment that eventually surfaces as friction — not because the side income itself was a bad idea, but because its actual cost was never made visible and agreed to up front.

The fix mirrors the client-facing structure in this chapter, applied at home instead: name the specific block out loud, to the specific person it affects, before it's already been happening for months. "I'm going to use Tuesday and Thursday evenings for the side business — can we figure out how that works with dinner and the kids' schedule?" is a five-minute conversation that prevents a much longer, harder one later. If the honest answer is that the household genuinely can't absorb the proposed block without real strain on someone else, that's important information the same way a primary-job strain signal is in Step 5 — it's a cue to negotiate a smaller block or a different arrangement, not a cue to proceed anyway and hope it works itself out.

What a bad week looks like, and how to recover from it

Even a well-structured time-boxing system, applied consistently for months, will occasionally meet a genuinely bad week — a sick child, a demanding stretch at the primary job, an unexpected personal emergency — where the normal block simply isn't available. The instinct in a bad week is often either to push through anyway, borrowing hours from sleep or from the primary job to protect the side income's normal pace, or to quietly abandon the structure altogether out of overwhelm. Neither serves you well.

The better response, built directly into the system this chapter describes, is a planned, temporary reduction: message any affected clients honestly and early — "I'm dealing with a family situation this week and will be a bit slower than usual to respond, back to normal by [specific date]" — rather than either overextending silently or going dark without explanation. Clients generally respond well to an honest, specific, time-bound update; what damages a relationship isn't the occasional bad week, it's an unexplained silence that leaves them guessing. Once the bad week passes, resume the normal block and hour ceiling exactly as before, rather than trying to make up the missed hours all at once the following week — a single rough patch, handled honestly and recovered from cleanly, does far less damage to a side income than a single rough patch handled by silently overextending until something breaks.

Deciding whether to grow the block over time

The specific weekly block set at the start of a side income isn't meant to stay fixed forever — as a business grows and proves itself, it's reasonable to consider expanding the block, and this chapter's discipline applies just as much to that decision as it did to the original one. The mistake to avoid is expanding the block reactively, hour by hour, in response to immediate pressure from a busy week, rather than deliberately, as a considered choice made with the same care as the original block was set.

A useful check before expanding: has the current block consistently produced work you're proud of, delivered without the boundary-slipping warning signs covered earlier in this chapter, for at least two or three consecutive months? If yes, a modest, specific expansion — one additional evening, an extra hour on an existing day — is a reasonable next step, decided deliberately rather than backed into. If the current block has already been showing strain, expanding it further compounds the underlying problem rather than solving it; the honest move in that case is addressing the strain first, through the scaling levers this book covers later, before adding more hours on top of a structure that isn't yet holding cleanly.

Chapter 6 — Sole Proprietor or LLC: The Structure Decision

What actually changes when you file paperwork, and what doesn't

The situation

A paralegal starts freelance resume-writing on the side, earning a modest but real amount within her first two months. A friend, hearing about it, tells her she needs to "form an LLC immediately or you're personally liable for everything." Alarmed, she spends a weekend researching LLC formation, gets overwhelmed by state filing fees, registered-agent requirements, and annual report obligations that seem disproportionate to the roughly $400 a month she's currently earning, and nearly abandons the whole side income out of paperwork anxiety before she's even confirmed whether any of it actually applies to her situation yet.

The mechanics

The sole-proprietorship-versus-LLC decision gets more anxious attention at the start of a side income than almost any other topic in this book, and most of that anxiety is disproportionate to the actual stakes at this specific stage. Here's the mechanical reality, plainly: if you do nothing at all, and you're earning money from a side activity under your own name, you are automatically a sole proprietor. No filing, no paperwork, no fee. This is the default state, not a choice you have to make — and for a genuinely early-stage side income with modest revenue and low personal liability risk, it's frequently the right structure to start with, not a mistake to be corrected in a panic.

An LLC — a limited liability company — exists to create a legal separation between your personal assets and your business's liabilities. If your business gets sued, or takes on debt it can't repay, an LLC structure is designed to shield your personal home, car, and savings from that liability in a way a sole proprietorship doesn't. This protection is real and matters — but it matters in direct proportion to your actual liability exposure, which varies enormously by the kind of work you do. A freelance resume writer has genuinely low liability exposure; the realistic worst case of a bad outcome is an unhappy client and a refund, not a lawsuit that threatens personal assets. A side business doing home repairs, giving financial or medical advice, or handling other people's property carries meaningfully higher liability exposure, and the calculus shifts accordingly, sooner.

There's also a cost side to this decision that gets underweighted in the panic that drives premature LLC formation: state filing fees, in many states, an annual report requirement with its own fee, and in some cases genuinely added tax complexity depending on how the LLC elects to be taxed. None of this is prohibitive once a side income is earning real, sustained money — but it's a real cost against a side income that's still earning a few hundred dollars a month, and paying it before it's needed is money that could otherwise be reinvested in the business itself.

It helps to say directly where the friend's alarmed advice in this chapter's opening scenario comes from, because it's a genuinely common piece of folk wisdom rather than a fringe misunderstanding: the sense that operating without an LLC is somehow reckless or unprofessional. This impression usually comes from hearing about LLC formation in the context of businesses with real, meaningful liability exposure — a contractor, a consultant giving high-stakes advice, a business taking on debt or investors — where the advice is genuinely correct. The mistake is applying that same urgency uniformly, regardless of the specific business's actual risk profile, rather than running the checklist in this chapter against your own situation and letting the answer follow from the actual exposure rather than from a general anxiety about being under-protected.

The script and framework

Step 1 — Start as a sole proprietor unless a specific, clear risk factor says otherwise. This is the default, requires no paperwork, and lets you focus your limited early hours on getting clients and delivering work rather than on business-formation administration. Track income and expenses cleanly from day one regardless of structure — this matters for Chapter 7 no matter which structure you choose.

Step 2 — Assess your actual liability exposure honestly, using a short checklist rather than a vague worry. Ask: could my work realistically cause a client physical harm or significant property damage? Am I giving advice (financial, medical, legal, or otherwise) where a mistake could produce a real, provable financial loss for the client? Am I regularly handling significant sums of client money or property? Will I be hiring anyone, even part-time, in the near future? A "yes" to any of these meaningfully raises the case for forming an LLC sooner rather than later, even at modest revenue. A "no" to all of them means the sole-proprietorship default is reasonable to stay with for now.

Step 3 — Set a revenue-based or risk-based trigger for revisiting the decision, rather than leaving it permanently unexamined. A common, reasonable trigger: revisit the decision once the side income is producing consistent monthly revenue in the low four figures, or the moment your liability checklist from Step 2 changes (you start hiring, you start handling significantly more client money or property, you take on a client whose scope carries genuinely higher risk than your earlier work). Write the trigger down so it's a scheduled decision, not something you only remember to think about during a moment of alarm.

Step 4 — When you do form an LLC, treat it as a real structural change, not a formality. Open a separate business bank account, keep business and personal funds genuinely separate from day one, and use the LLC's name on contracts and invoices going forward — an LLC that shares a bank account with your personal finances offers meaningfully weaker real protection than one where the separation is clean and consistently maintained, a distinction courts do look at when a liability shield is actually tested.

Step 5 — Keep a copy of your reasoning, not just your decision. Whichever structure you land on, write a short, dated note to yourself explaining the specific answers that led to it — which liability questions were yes or no, what revenue you were at, what your trigger for revisiting is. Six months or a year later, when the question resurfaces, this note lets you evaluate whether anything has actually changed rather than re-litigating the entire decision from scratch, or worse, making a new decision based on whatever anxiety happens to be loudest that particular week.

Worked example

The paralegal runs the liability checklist honestly. Resume writing doesn't involve physical risk, doesn't create provable financial loss from an honest mistake beyond an unhappy client, doesn't involve handling significant client money beyond a modest project fee, and she has no plans to hire anyone soon. She decides, calmly rather than anxiously, to operate as a sole proprietor for now, and instead spends the weekend she'd nearly lost to LLC-formation panic setting up a simple, separate system for tracking her business income and expenses — which turns out to matter far more immediately than business structure does at her current stage.

She sets her revisit trigger at $1,500 in consistent monthly revenue, sustained for three months, and writes a note in her calendar six months out to check in on it regardless. By the time she crosses that threshold seven months later, she forms an LLC in an afternoon, using her state's standard online filing process, opens a dedicated business bank account the same week, and moves all client invoicing to the new entity's name going forward — a clean, deliberate transition rather than the anxious, premature one she nearly made before she'd earned a single dollar.

A second worked example

A landscaper starting a side business mowing and maintaining yards for neighbors and small local properties runs the same liability checklist and gets a very different set of answers than the paralegal did. Physical risk is real — mowing equipment, ladders for gutter work, and regular presence on other people's property all carry genuine potential for property damage or injury. There's no financial-advice exposure, but there is meaningful potential for a damaged fence, a severed sprinkler line, or an injury on someone else's lawn. He isn't planning to hire anyone yet, but he is regularly handling client property in the literal sense of working on it directly.

Two "yes" answers on the checklist — physical risk and regular work on client property — meaningfully change his calculus compared to the paralegal's clean sweep of "no" answers. Rather than waiting for a revenue trigger the way she did, he decides the risk profile itself justifies forming an LLC earlier, even at modest early revenue, and pairs it with a general liability insurance policy sized for a small landscaping operation — the insurance-as-complement point raised at the end of this chapter, applied directly to a case where it clearly matters. He also keeps a written incident log from his very first job onward, noting anything unusual (a rock kicked up near a window, a client's dog getting loose during a visit) even when nothing came of it, since a documented history of careful practice is itself a meaningful piece of protection if a real claim ever does arise.

A note on liability insurance as a complement, not a substitute

For side incomes with real liability exposure — anything involving physical work in someone else's home, advice with financial consequences, or handling client property — a modest liability insurance policy is frequently a more immediately useful protection than business structure alone, and it's worth researching alongside, not instead of, the sole-proprietor-versus-LLC decision. Structure and insurance solve overlapping but distinct problems, and a side income with meaningful risk exposure is often best served by both eventually, rather than treating either one as sufficient on its own.

Common objections and how to handle them

"Doesn't operating as a sole proprietor mean I'm not really running a real business?" No — the legal structure has no bearing on whether the business is real. A sole proprietorship is a fully legitimate, fully legal way to run a business, used by a large share of small, early-stage businesses in the country, and it comes with real obligations of its own, including the tax responsibilities covered in the next chapter. "Real business" is a function of whether you're delivering real value for real payment, not a function of which state filing you've completed.

"What about a business name — do I need to register one even as a sole proprietor?" Depending on your state, operating under a name other than your own legal name — "Riverside Home Tune-Ups" instead of your own name — typically requires a separate, usually inexpensive filing, often called a DBA ("doing business as") or fictitious business name registration, distinct from forming an LLC. This is a much smaller step than full LLC formation and is worth checking with your state or county's specific requirements if you plan to operate under a business name from the start.

"What if I'm not sure whether my specific work counts as higher liability risk?" When genuinely unsure, a brief, low-cost consultation with a local attorney or a business advisor through your state's Small Business Development Center — a free, federally supported resource available in every state — is a reasonable way to get a specific answer for your specific situation, rather than guessing from a general framework alone. The checklist in this chapter is a starting filter, not a substitute for professional judgment on an edge case that matters to you.

Frequently misunderstood point: an LLC doesn't eliminate personal responsibility for your own actions

A common misconception worth correcting directly: forming an LLC protects your personal assets from the business's liabilities, but it does not shield you personally from liability for your own direct negligence — if you personally cause harm through carelessness, an LLC structure generally doesn't erase your personal responsibility for that specific act, even though it still protects your personal assets from most other business-related claims and debts. This is exactly why the liability insurance discussed later in this chapter matters as a genuine complement to structure rather than a redundant extra step — insurance and entity structure cover meaningfully different kinds of exposure, and a side income with real physical or advisory risk benefits from understanding both rather than assuming an LLC alone closes the loop.

A note on business licenses and local permits

Separate from the sole-proprietor-versus-LLC decision, many cities and counties require a general business license or a specific trade permit for certain kinds of work, regardless of your business's legal structure — this is a local requirement, not a federal or state entity-formation issue, and it's easy to overlook because it doesn't come up in most general business-structure guidance. Check your specific city and county's requirements early, particularly for any side income involving in-home services, food preparation, or a physical storefront or booth, since operating without a required local license can carry real fines even when your federal tax filing and entity structure are both handled correctly.

A full conversation, start to finish

The liability assessment from this chapter, worked through out loud, looks something like this — a version of the internal conversation worth having with yourself, or with a partner, before deciding.

"Could my work realistically cause physical harm or real property damage?" — For the paralegal's resume writing, no. For the landscaper's mowing and gutter work, yes, meaningfully.

"Am I giving advice where a mistake could cause a provable financial loss?" — For the resume writer, arguably a weak yes — a badly written resume could theoretically cost someone an opportunity — but it's a low, hard-to-prove kind of exposure. For the landscaper, no, this specific question doesn't apply to his work.

"Am I regularly handling significant client money or property?" — Neither the paralegal nor the landscaper handles

significant client money, though the landscaper is regularly present on and working directly on client property.

"Will I be hiring anyone soon?" — No, for both, at least for now.

Run side by side, the same four questions produce two different, reasonable conclusions: the paralegal reasonably stays a sole proprietor for now, and the landscaper reasonably moves toward an LLC and insurance sooner, even at similar early revenue. The checklist doesn't produce a universal answer — it produces the right answer for the specific risk profile in front of it, which is exactly what it's built to do.

A short exercise before you move to Chapter 7

Run the four-question liability checklist from Step 2 against your specific offer right now, answering honestly rather than optimistically. Write down your answer to each question, your decision (sole proprietor or LLC), and your specific revisit trigger from Step 3 with an actual number and an actual date attached. This isn't a decision to make once in your head and forget — it's a decision worth having in writing, the same way your pricing graduation trigger from Chapter 3 is, so that revisiting it later is a scheduled check rather than a moment of sudden alarm.

What changes once you bring on your first subcontractor or employee

Everything in this chapter up to this point assumes a solo operation, but Chapter 9's scaling framework will eventually raise the possibility of delegation for a genuinely growing side income, and it's worth flagging now what shifts once that happens, since it interacts directly with the structure decision covered here. Hiring a subcontractor — a freelancer paid for a specific, defined piece of work, responsible for their own taxes — is a meaningfully lower-complexity step than hiring an employee, and it's the more common first move for a side income adding help. It still comes with real obligations worth understanding in advance: proper classification matters, since misclassifying an employee as a subcontractor to avoid payroll obligations is a real compliance risk, not a gray area to guess at casually, and the IRS's own worker-classification guidance is worth reviewing directly before making the call on a specific working relationship.

Bringing on even one subcontractor is also, on its own, a reasonable trigger to revisit the sole-proprietor-versus-LLC decision from this chapter, regardless of where your revenue-based trigger from Step 3 currently sits — the liability profile of a business directing someone else's work is genuinely different from one where you're the only person performing the work, and the checklist in this chapter should be rerun with that change explicitly factored in rather than assumed away.

Revisiting the decision as the business and the law both change

The sole-proprietor-versus-LLC decision in this chapter isn't a single, permanent choice made once and never touched again — it's a decision that deserves revisiting for two separate reasons over time, and it's worth distinguishing between them. The first is the business-side trigger this chapter already covers: revenue growth, new hires, or a change in the actual risk profile of the work. The second, less obvious reason is that the legal and tax landscape around entity structure — state filing fees, LLC tax election options, liability standards — shifts periodically at both the federal and state level, independent of anything about your specific business.

A reasonable habit, once a structure decision has been made, is a brief, once-a-year check — not a full reconsideration, just a quick confirmation that nothing material has changed either in your business's risk profile or in your state's specific requirements for the structure you're operating under. This is a small, low-effort habit compared to the cost of operating for years under a structure that quietly stopped fitting your actual situation, whether because the business grew past its original assumptions or because a specific state requirement changed in a way that now applies to you.

Chapter 7 — Quarterly Estimated Taxes Without an Accountant

Keeping what you owe set aside so April never surprises you

The situation

An airline gate agent starts a small pet-sitting and dog-walking side business, earning around $600 a month by the end of her first year. She's never thought about taxes on it beyond a vague plan to "deal with it in April," treating the side income the same way she treats her regular paycheck, where taxes are simply withheld automatically before the money ever reaches her. In February, doing her taxes, she learns two things at once: she owes self-employment tax on top of ordinary income tax on every dollar of that side income, and because she never made estimated payments during the year, she owes a penalty on top of the tax itself, for underpaying throughout a year she didn't realize required active management at all.

The mechanics

The single biggest tax surprise for a first-time side-income earner isn't the tax rate — it's the fact that side income requires active management throughout the year, in a way a regular paycheck never demanded. A W-2 paycheck has income tax, Social Security, and Medicare withheld automatically by an employer before the money ever reaches you. Side income, by default, has nothing withheld at all — the full responsibility for setting money aside and paying it on the correct schedule sits entirely with you.

Two separate tax obligations apply to self-employment income, and it's worth understanding them as genuinely distinct pieces rather than one vague "self-employment tax" concept. The first is ordinary income tax, at your normal marginal rate, exactly as it would apply to any other income you earn. The second is self-employment tax, which covers the Social Security and Medicare contributions that an employer would otherwise split with you on a W-2 job — as a self-employed person, you owe both halves, which is why the self-employment tax rate is meaningfully higher than the employee-side payroll tax rate most people are used to seeing on a regular pay stub. Current rates and thresholds for both are set by the IRS and are worth verifying directly at irs.gov, since they're adjusted periodically.

The penalty the gate agent encountered isn't a punishment for owing tax — it's a penalty specifically for underpaying throughout the year rather than paying on the IRS's required schedule. The federal tax system operates on a pay-as-you-go basis: it expects tax to be paid as income is earned, not settled entirely at filing time, which is exactly what automatic withholding does for a W-2 employee and exactly what nobody is doing for a side-income earner unless they set it up themselves. Quarterly estimated payments exist to replicate, manually, the same pay-as-you-go rhythm a paycheck's withholding does automatically.

There's a psychological dimension to this mechanic that's worth spelling out plainly, because it explains why the gate agent's mistake is so common rather than a sign of carelessness. A side-income payment arrives looking exactly like spendable money — a deposit, a check, a transfer — with no visible marker distinguishing the portion that's genuinely yours from the portion that already, functionally, belongs to a future tax bill.

A W-2 paycheck never presents this problem, because the withheld portion is subtracted before the deposit ever happens, so the number in the account has never included it in the first place. Side income requires manufacturing that same distinction yourself, mentally and mechanically, and the set-aside habit in Step 1 exists specifically to recreate the invisible subtraction a paycheck does automatically — treating the set-aside percentage as never having been available to spend, from the very first payment onward, rather than as a bill to be paid later out of money that's already been mentally spent.

The script and framework

Step 1 — Set aside a fixed percentage of every side-income payment the moment it arrives, into a separate account you don't touch for anything else. A commonly used starting estimate is 25 to 30 percent of gross side income, covering both self-employment tax and ordinary income tax at a moderate bracket — this is a rough planning figure, not a precise calculation, and your actual correct percentage depends on your total income, filing status, and bracket, which is worth confirming with the IRS's own estimated-tax worksheet (Form

1040-ES) or a tax professional once your side income becomes substantial. The mechanical habit matters more at first than precision: money set aside automatically, the moment it's earned, never has to be found later under pressure.

Step 2 — Learn the quarterly due dates and treat them as fixed obligations, not optional check-ins. The IRS's quarterly estimated payment deadlines fall in mid-April, mid-June, mid-September, and mid-January of the following year — the exact dates shift slightly year to year based on weekends and holidays, so confirm the current year's dates directly at irs.gov rather than assuming last year's schedule repeats exactly. Put all four dates in your calendar for the full year at once, at the start of your side income, rather than discovering each one as it approaches.

Step 3 — Use the IRS safe-harbor rule to know exactly how much you need to pay to avoid a penalty, without needing to calculate your exact final tax bill in advance. The safe harbor rule, as set by the IRS, generally protects you from an underpayment penalty if your total withholding and estimated payments across the year equal at least 90 percent of your current year's tax bill or 100 percent of your prior year's tax bill (110 percent if your prior year's income was above a certain threshold), whichever is smaller — verify the current thresholds directly, since they're part of federal tax law and set by the IRS, not something this book can guarantee stays fixed. In practice, for most first-time side-income earners with a stable primary job, matching the prior year's total tax liability through combined withholding and estimated payments is the simplest safe-harbor target to calculate and hit.

Step 4 — Track income and expenses continuously, not in a scramble each quarter. A simple spreadsheet or a basic bookkeeping tool, updated weekly or after every job, turns the quarterly estimated-payment calculation from a stressful research project into a five-minute task: total income for the quarter, total legitimate business expenses, apply your set-aside percentage, submit the payment. Legitimate business expenses — supplies, mileage for business use, a portion of relevant equipment — reduce your actual taxable income, and the IRS's own Schedule C instructions and Publication 334 lay out what qualifies in detail.

Step 5 — If your primary job offers it, consider using extra W-2 withholding as an alternative to some or all of the quarterly payments. Because W-2 withholding is treated by the IRS as having been paid evenly throughout the year regardless of when it's actually withheld, increasing your primary job's withholding late in the year can sometimes cover a side-income tax gap more simply than a separate quarterly payment process — this is a legitimate, commonly used strategy worth discussing with a tax professional if your situation is stable and predictable enough to make it work cleanly.

Taken together, these five steps convert an entire year's tax obligation from a single, dreaded event into a series of small, routine actions spread evenly across twelve months — a percentage set aside per payment, four dates already on the calendar, a known target to hit, ten minutes of tracking a week, and one strategic decision about withholding made once and revisited annually. None of the five steps is individually difficult; the difficulty most first-time side-income earners run into is skipping the system entirely and trying to reconstruct a full year's obligation from memory in the final weeks before filing, which is exactly the scramble this structure exists to prevent.

Worked example

The pet-sitting business owner, after her surprising first-year tax bill, sets up a dedicated savings account labeled specifically for taxes and moves 28 percent of every client payment into it immediately upon receipt, treating it as money that was never really hers to spend in the first place. She puts all four of the coming year's estimated payment deadlines into her phone's calendar with two-week advance reminders. She tracks her income and mileage in a simple spreadsheet, updated every Sunday evening in about ten minutes, logging each job's payment and any relevant expense — dog food she provides, mileage between client homes, a portion of a new leash and harness set purchased specifically for the business.

By her second year's first quarterly deadline, the payment calculation takes her about fifteen minutes: total quarterly income from her spreadsheet, minus tracked expenses, times her set-aside percentage, submitted through the IRS's online payment system before the deadline. She hits her safe-harbor target for the full year without needing to calculate her exact final tax liability in advance, and the following April, for the first time, her tax filing produces no surprise and no penalty — just a confirmation that the amount she'd already set aside and paid throughout the year was close to correct.

A second worked example

A court reporter with an established full-time position starts taking occasional freelance transcription jobs for a legal-services company on the side, earning irregular amounts month to month — sometimes $200, sometimes $900, depending on how much overflow work the company has. The variability makes a flat quarterly estimate feel like guesswork to her, so rather than a flat percentage applied evenly across the year, she uses the IRS's annualized income installment method described in Publication 505, calculating her actual estimated payment each quarter based on what she genuinely earned in that specific period rather than an even one-fourth split.

This requires more diligent tracking than a flat-percentage approach — she logs every job's payment the day it arrives, in a simple spreadsheet organized by quarter rather than by month — but it produces a materially fairer result for her specific situation: a slow quarter produces a smaller estimated payment, and a busy quarter produces a larger one, rather than either overpaying during a lean stretch or underpaying during a strong one and scrambling to catch up. She still sets aside her full percentage from every individual payment as it arrives, exactly as the pet-sitting business owner does — the annualized method changes how she calculates each quarterly payment, not whether she sets money aside consistently in the first place.

Common objections and how to handle them

"What if my side income is small — do I really need to bother with quarterly payments?" The IRS generally requires estimated payments once you expect to owe a meaningful amount of tax beyond what's covered by withholding — the specific threshold is set by the IRS and worth confirming directly, but a common rule of thumb is that if you expect to owe $1,000 or more in tax beyond your withholding for the year, quarterly payments apply. Even below that threshold, the set-aside habit from Step 1 is worth building early, since a small side income rarely stays small forever, and the habit is far easier to build before it matters than to retrofit once it does.

"Can I just wait and pay everything at once in April instead?" You can choose to do this, but it isn't free — if your total year's underpayment exceeds the safe-harbor thresholds in Step 3, the IRS applies a penalty calculated on the underpaid amount for each period it was outstanding, which is exactly the surprise the gate agent in this chapter's opening ran into. Paying quarterly, on schedule, at the safe-harbor level isn't optional caution — it's the mechanism that avoids a specific, calculable cost.

"What if my side income varies a lot month to month — how do I estimate a consistent quarterly payment?" For a genuinely variable side income, the IRS's annualized income installment method, detailed in Publication 505, allows estimated payments to be calculated based on actual income earned in each specific period rather than a flat even split across the year — useful for a seasonal or highly irregular side income where a flat quarterly estimate would either overpay early in a slow season or underpay during a sudden busy one. This method requires more careful tracking than the flat-percentage approach in this chapter, but it's worth understanding if your income genuinely doesn't arrive on an even keel.

Frequently misunderstood point: self-employment tax isn't a penalty for being self-employed

It's a common and understandable reaction to feel that self-employment tax is somehow an unfair extra charge for choosing to earn side income rather than working a second W-2 job. It isn't an extra charge — it's the same Social Security and Medicare contribution every worker makes, restructured to reflect that a self-employed person doesn't have an employer splitting that contribution with them the way a W-2 job does. A W-2 employee's paycheck already has this same total contribution taken out, half from the employee and half matched silently by the employer, so it never shows up as a single visible number the way self-employment tax does on a self-employed person's return. Self-employment tax is more visible, not more punitive — the total contribution is comparable, and the visibility is exactly why the set-aside habit in this chapter matters so much: nobody is doing it invisibly on your behalf anymore.

A note on state income tax

Everything in this chapter addresses federal tax obligations specifically, but most states with a state income tax impose their own estimated-payment requirements on self-employment income, on a broadly similar quarterly schedule but with their own separate forms, thresholds, and payment portals. If you live in a state with income tax, check your specific state revenue department's website for its own estimated-tax requirements — the federal safe-harbor logic in this chapter doesn't automatically satisfy a separate state-level obligation, and treating the two as one combined requirement is a common and avoidable oversight.

A note on what counts as a deductible business expense

The set-aside percentage in this chapter is applied against gross income minus legitimate business expenses, which makes an honest, well-organized accounting of those expenses directly valuable — every properly documented expense lowers the actual tax owed, not just the paperwork burden. Common categories worth tracking from day one, per the IRS's own Schedule C and Publication 334 guidance: supplies and materials used directly in delivering the offer, a portion of a vehicle's mileage when driving specifically for business purposes (tracked contemporaneously, not reconstructed later from memory), a reasonable portion of a phone or internet bill when genuinely used for the business, and any tools or equipment purchased specifically to deliver the work. The common mistake in this category runs in both directions — either failing to track legitimate expenses at all and overpaying as a result, or claiming expenses with a genuinely personal, not business, purpose, which is exactly the kind of claim that draws scrutiny if a return is ever examined. When a specific expense's business-versus-personal nature is genuinely unclear, the IRS's own guidance and a tax professional are the right places to resolve it, not a guess made in the moment of filing.

A short exercise before you move to Chapter 8

Open a separate savings account today, if you haven't already, and label it specifically for taxes. Set your percentage — 25 to 30 percent as a reasonable starting estimate, refined later against the IRS's own worksheets once you have more data — and move that percentage of your very next side-income payment into it immediately upon receipt. Put all four of the current year's quarterly deadlines into your calendar right now, with a two-week advance reminder on each. This is the entire mechanical core of this chapter, reduced to four concrete actions you can complete in the next twenty minutes.

A simple first-year tax calendar

For anyone starting entirely from scratch, it helps to see the whole first year laid out as a single sequence rather than a set of separate rules to remember independently. In the first week of side income: open the dedicated tax savings account, set the percentage, and begin the weekly income-and-expense log described in Step 4. Before the first quarterly deadline (mid-April for income earned January through March): calculate the quarter's set-aside using the flat-percentage method, submit the payment through the IRS's online system, and note the confirmation for your records. Before the second and third deadlines (mid-June and mid-September): repeat the same calculation and submission, updating the running log each time rather than starting from scratch. Before the fourth and final deadline for the tax year (mid-January of the following year): repeat once more, and use this moment to take stock of the full year's income and expenses in preparation for filing. At tax filing time (by mid-April of the following year): file the actual return using the full year's tracked income and expenses, reconcile it against what was already paid through the four quarterly payments, and use any gap between what you paid and what you actually owed to refine next year's set-aside percentage.

This same five-checkpoint structure repeats every year with growing ease, since each year's log and each year's filed return becomes a more accurate reference point for calibrating the next year's set-aside percentage — the entire system gets more precise with use, not just more familiar.

What to do if you fall behind

The system in this chapter works best applied from the start, but it's honest to address directly what to do if you're reading this partway through a year having made no estimated payments and kept no consistent tracking. The first move is the same regardless of how far behind you are: start the set-aside habit immediately, on your very next payment, rather than waiting for a "clean" starting point that doesn't actually exist. A partial year of good practice is meaningfully better than continuing to wait for an ideal moment to begin.

Second, reconstruct what you can of the year so far — bank deposits, invoices sent, any record of client payments — well enough to estimate a reasonable catch-up payment at the next available quarterly deadline, even if it's imperfect. An imperfect but genuine estimate submitted on the next deadline is better than perfect precision achieved only in April. Third, if the gap is significant or the situation feels genuinely unclear, a single paid consultation with a tax professional at this point is a reasonable, worthwhile expense — not a sign of failure, but the appropriate tool for a specific, complicated catch-up situation that a general framework like this chapter's isn't built to resolve down to the last dollar. Falling behind on this system is common, correctable, and considerably less costly to fix now than to keep avoiding.

A note on filing software versus a tax professional

For a genuinely simple side income — a single offer, straightforward expenses, no employees or subcontractors — reputable tax preparation software that specifically supports Schedule C and self-employment income is often sufficient for filing an accurate return without engaging a professional, and it typically walks through the relevant deductions and calculations in a guided way that reduces the risk of missing something. As the business grows in complexity — multiple income streams, meaningful equipment depreciation, an entity structure beyond a simple sole proprietorship, employees or regular subcontractors — the case for a paid tax professional strengthens accordingly, both for the accuracy of the return itself and for proactive guidance on decisions like the entity-structure questions covered in Chapter 6.

There's no fixed revenue threshold at which one clearly becomes correct and the other clearly becomes wrong — it's a judgment call based on the actual complexity of your specific situation, not the size of the number on the bottom line. A useful gut check: if your filing would take more than a rough hour or two to complete carefully with guided software, or if you find yourself genuinely unsure how to categorize more than one or two specific transactions, that uncertainty is itself the signal that a professional's judgment is worth the cost for at least that year's return.

Chapter 8 — Reinvest or Pay Yourself: The Cash Allocation Decision

A framework for deciding where every dollar of side income actually goes

The situation

A retail assistant manager's social-media-management side business, run for small local businesses in her area, grows from a single client to five within a year, and she suddenly finds herself with more monthly side income than she's ever had to make a deliberate decision about before. Every dollar that comes in gets spent the same way, without much thought: some goes into general household spending, some quietly disappears into things she can't fully account for by month's end, and none of it goes toward anything that would help the business grow faster or run more smoothly. The business is working. The money from it isn't being used with any intention at all.

The mechanics

Once a side income starts producing real, recurring revenue, every dollar it generates faces a genuine allocation decision, whether or not that decision gets made consciously: pay yourself now, reinvest in the business's future capacity, or set the money aside for the tax and structural obligations covered in the previous two chapters. Treating all side-income revenue as identical to a regular paycheck — spendable the moment it arrives — skips this decision by default, and the default answer is almost never the right one, because it treats every dollar as already fully "earned" in a way business revenue actually isn't until taxes and reasonable reinvestment have been accounted for first.

The reinvest-versus-pay-yourself tension isn't really a binary choice between two options — it's a three-way split, and the tax set-aside from Chapter 7 has to come off the top before either of the other two questions even gets asked, since that money was never really available to allocate in the first place. What's left after the tax set-aside is the genuine decision point: how much goes toward building the business's future capacity to earn more (better tools, wider marketing reach, a course or certification that unlocks higher-value work, eventually help from another person), and how much goes toward paying yourself now, as real, spendable income for the actual hours you put in.

There's no single universally correct split, but there is a useful mechanical principle: the right split shifts systematically as the business matures. In the earliest stage, when the offer and the client-acquisition process are still unproven, a larger share of any profit reasonably goes toward reinvestment — proving the offer works, building the basic tools and systems the business needs to run smoothly, and covering the parts of Chapters 6 and 7 that protect it structurally. As the business matures into a proven, repeatable pattern with reliable clients, the split can reasonably shift toward paying yourself more, because the marginal value of additional reinvestment starts to decline while the value of being compensated for real, ongoing hours worked stays constant or grows.

The retail manager's situation in this chapter's opening illustrates a specific failure mode that deserves calling out directly: money that never gets deliberately allocated doesn't disappear into nothing — it defaults into whichever spending happens to be nearest at hand, usually general household expenses, without ever being evaluated against what it could have done for the business or for a genuine, tracked personal benefit. This is a different problem from underpricing or poor client acquisition; the business itself was working exactly as intended, generating real revenue from real clients. What was missing wasn't the income — it was a decision layer sitting between the income arriving and the income being spent, the same kind of decision layer a well-run company applies automatically and a side income has to build for itself on purpose.

The script and framework

Step 1 — Set aside the tax percentage from Chapter 7 first, automatically, before any other allocation decision. This isn't optional and isn't part of the reinvest-versus-pay-yourself split — it's money that was never fully yours to allocate, and treating it otherwise is what produces the tax surprises this book already covered in the previous chapter.

Step 2 — Assess your current stage honestly, using three questions. Is your offer proven — do you have a repeatable process that reliably produces paying clients, or are you still testing what works? Do you have the basic tools and systems the business needs to run efficiently, or are inefficiencies still costing you real time and money? Are you currently turning down real, viable work because of a capacity limit — Chapter 5's hour ceiling, a lack of a specific tool, or a skill gap — that reinvestment could directly address?

Step 3 — Set a starting split based on your honest answers, and revisit it on a fixed schedule rather than by feel. A reasonable starting point for a genuinely early-stage business, still proving its offer and building basic tools: 60 percent reinvestment, 40 percent pay-yourself, on top of the tax set-aside. A reasonable range for a matured, proven business with reliable clients and no major capacity constraints: 20 percent reinvestment, 80 percent pay-yourself. Neither number is a rule — they're starting points to adjust against your specific situation, revisited monthly or quarterly rather than left to drift by default.

Step 4 — Make every reinvestment specific and justified, not vague. "Reinvesting in the business" as a general category is how reinvestment money quietly turns into unaccounted spending with nothing to show for it. Every reinvestment dollar should have a specific target — a specific tool, a specific piece of training, a specific marketing effort — with a rough expectation of what it should produce, so you can actually evaluate afterward whether it worked.

Step 5 — Pay yourself deliberately, on a schedule, rather than absorbing side income invisibly into general spending. Moving your pay-yourself allocation into your regular personal account on a fixed schedule — monthly, for most side incomes — makes it feel like real, earned income rather than found money, which in turn makes it easier to actually notice and value the work you're doing, rather than having it disappear untracked into the household budget the way the retail manager's income initially did.

A useful habit to attach to this five-step process: at the same moment you set your split each quarter, write one sentence describing what stage the business is in and why the split is set where it is. Read that sentence back at the next quarterly check-in before deciding whether to change anything. This turns the allocation decision into a running record you can actually learn from over time, rather than a number reset from scratch, by feel, every few months with no memory of the reasoning behind the last one.

Worked example

The social-media manager, after five months of unstructured spending, sits down and honestly assesses her stage: her offer is proven — five clients, consistent renewals, a repeatable onboarding process — but she's turning down two viable prospects a month because she's at her hour ceiling from Chapter 5, and a basic scheduling tool she's been meaning to buy would meaningfully cut the hours her current process takes per client. She sets a 45/55 split, reinvestment to pay-yourself, on top of her existing 25 percent tax set-aside.

Her first specific reinvestment: a $30-a-month content scheduling tool that cuts roughly ninety minutes a week off her current process — a specific, testable bet rather than a vague "invest in the business" line item. Three months later, she evaluates it honestly: the tool delivered close to the expected time savings, freeing up capacity for one additional client without raising her weekly hour ceiling. She takes on that sixth client, reassesses her split at her next quarterly check-in, and shifts it to 30/70 as her process matures further, moving her pay-yourself allocation into her personal checking account on the first of every month rather than letting it blend invisibly into her existing spending the way her earlier, unstructured income had.

A second worked example

A home inspector building a side business doing pre-listing inspections for local real estate agents faces a different allocation question than the social media manager's process-efficiency problem: his limiting factor is entirely equipment. A more capable moisture meter and a proper thermal imaging attachment for his phone would let him offer a more thorough inspection and justify a meaningfully higher price, but together they cost more than a single month of his current side-income profit.

He runs the same three-question assessment: his offer is proven, with steady referrals from two agents already, but his current tool set genuinely limits what he can credibly inspect and charge for — a capacity and quality problem, not a hour-ceiling problem the way the photographer's or the social media manager's turned out to be. He sets an aggressive early-stage split of 70 percent reinvestment, 30 percent pay-yourself, on top of his tax set-aside, specifically because the equipment purchase is a one-time cost with a clear, calculable payoff — he can name the specific new inspection tier and price increase the equipment would unlock before he ever buys it. He saves toward the full equipment cost over two months rather than financing it, buys both pieces in the same month once the reinvestment bucket covers it, and shifts his split back down to a more typical 25/75 the following quarter, once the one-time purchase is behind him and the ongoing business no longer has a specific, named gap to fund.

Common objections and how to handle them

"What if I need every dollar of my side income for personal expenses right now?" This is a real and common situation, and it doesn't mean the framework in this chapter doesn't apply — it means your current pay-yourself allocation is legitimately closer to 90 or even 100 percent of what's left after taxes, with minimal reinvestment until your personal financial situation has more room. That's a valid starting split for a specific, honest reason. What matters is that the decision is made deliberately, at a chosen percentage, rather than by default — and that you revisit it once your situation allows, rather than leaving it permanently at 100 percent out of habit long after the original reason has passed.

"How do I know if a reinvestment actually worked?" Attach a specific, measurable expectation to every reinvestment before you spend the money, as the social media manager did with her scheduling tool — a specific number of hours saved, a specific increase in capacity, a specific improvement you can check for afterward. A reinvestment without a stated expectation is nearly impossible to evaluate honestly later, because there's nothing concrete to measure the outcome against.

"Should I ever reinvest in something with a less certain, longer-term payoff, like a certification or a course?" Yes, and it's worth treating this category slightly differently from a concrete tool purchase — a certification or a skill-building course is a reasonable reinvestment when it unlocks a specific, identifiable higher-value offer you couldn't credibly sell without it, not simply because it sounds generally useful. Before committing reinvestment funds to this category, write down the specific new offer or price tier the credential would unlock, and treat that as the measurable expectation the same way a tool purchase gets one.

Frequently misunderstood point: paying yourself isn't the same as spending carelessly

It's tempting to read the pay-yourself half of this chapter's split as simply "whatever's left after taxes and reinvestment, spend freely" — but that framing misses what makes the allocation actually useful. Paying yourself, done well, means moving a deliberate amount into your personal accounts on a fixed schedule and then treating it the same way you'd treat any other earned income in your broader financial plan — some spent, some saved, some directed toward whatever goals your personal finances already call for. The point of separating it out isn't to license unstructured spending; it's to make the side income's earnings visible and real, rather than letting them dissolve invisibly into a blended pool of business and personal money the way the retail manager's income did before she built this framework.

A note on emergency reserves as a fourth bucket

Beyond taxes, reinvestment, and pay-yourself, a side income that's become a meaningful and consistent part of your household finances benefits from a fourth allocation: a small business emergency reserve, separate from your personal emergency fund, sized to cover a slow month or an unexpected business expense — a broken tool, a canceled contract, a client who pays late — without disrupting either your tax set-aside or your personal spending. A modest reserve, built gradually at a small percentage of the reinvestment or pay-yourself bucket until it reaches one to two months of typical business expenses, absorbs exactly the kind of volatility that Chapter 10 asks you to measure honestly before ever considering the business as a primary income.

A full allocation conversation, walked through step by step

It helps to see the allocation decision reasoned through out loud, rather than only as an abstract split. Here is the social media manager's actual thinking, laid out in order, once she sat down to fix her unstructured spending.

"First, what's already spoken for?" Twenty-five percent, off the top, into the tax account — untouchable, not part of the real decision.

"What's left, and what stage am I actually at?" Her offer is proven, five renewing clients, but she's turning away real, viable work because of her hour ceiling, and a specific tool exists that would recover some of those lost hours.

"So what's the split?" Forty-five percent of what's left toward reinvestment — enough to genuinely fund the tool and leave room for a second, smaller experiment later — fifty-five percent toward paying herself now, since she's also been running the business on unpaid effort for five months and that imbalance needs correcting too.

"When do I revisit this?" Quarterly, on a fixed calendar date, not "whenever it feels relevant" — a date she can hold herself to regardless of how busy a given month gets.

Walking through the decision in this order — obligation first, honest stage assessment second, specific split third, a scheduled revisit fourth — turns what could be an anxious, circular question into a short, mechanical sequence with a clear answer at the end of it.

A short exercise before you move to Chapter 9

Look at your side income's revenue from the last full month. Apply your tax set-aside first, then honestly answer the three stage-assessment questions from Step 2, then write your starting split — a specific percentage, not a vague intention — for reinvestment versus pay-yourself. Move the pay-yourself portion into your personal account today, on purpose, rather than letting it sit blended with your business funds. That single transfer, done deliberately, is what turns a side income's earnings from background noise in your finances into something you actually notice and can evaluate.

How the split changes once a side income supports real household expenses

The reinvest-versus-pay-yourself split in this chapter describes the standard case, where the pay-yourself portion functions as discretionary personal income. But once a side income grows enough to genuinely factor into covering fixed household expenses — part of a mortgage or rent payment, a portion of childcare, a real and regular contribution to the family budget rather than extra spending money — the calculation deserves an added layer of caution before continuing to reinvest aggressively.

Specifically, before committing to a reinvestment-heavy split once a side income is relied upon this way, run the volatility check that Chapter 10 introduces for a full income-replacement decision, at a smaller scale: look at your worst month, not your average, and confirm that even a lean month's pay-yourself allocation still covers whatever fixed obligation now depends on it. A business that's genuinely become a load-bearing part of household finances needs its pay-yourself allocation treated with the same seriousness as

Chapter 10's replacement-income runway, even if the business is still meaningfully smaller than a full income replacement — the household doesn't experience the difference between "a growing side income" and "a full income" gradually; it experiences the difference the first month a relied-upon payment doesn't show up as expected.

A note on business credit and financing

Reinvestment doesn't always need to come entirely from current profit — for a specific, well-justified purchase with a clear payoff, financed through a business credit card or a small business loan, borrowing can occasionally make sense. It's worth being disciplined about when this is genuinely reasonable versus when it's simply postponing the honest allocation decision this chapter is built around. A reasonable case for financing: a specific piece of equipment with a clear, calculable payoff timeline, similar to the home inspector's equipment purchase earlier in this chapter, where financing lets the reinvestment happen sooner without waiting to save the full amount, and the expected revenue increase clearly covers the financing cost. An unreasonable case: financing ongoing operating expenses or a vaguely justified "growth" purchase with no specific expected return, which is a sign the business's actual cash flow doesn't yet support the ambition behind the purchase, and financing it only delays that reckoning rather than resolving it.

If you do use a business credit card, keep it entirely separate from personal credit — a business-specific card supports the clean bookkeeping this book has emphasized throughout, and it keeps a business debt from silently becoming difficult to distinguish from personal debt if the business's fortunes change.

Chapter 9 — Scaling Without Burning Out

Raising prices, raising capacity, or adding help — and how to choose

The situation

A veterinary technician's mobile pet-photography side business, started as a modest weekend project, becomes genuinely popular within its first year — word of mouth from happy clients produces more demand than she can currently handle inside her existing hours. Her instinct, facing more demand than capacity, is to simply say yes to everyone and work harder to fit it all in. Within two months of doing exactly that, she's exhausted, her actual full-time job is starting to suffer the way Chapter 5 warned about, and the quality of her photography — the thing that made the business work in the first place — has started to visibly decline under the compressed schedule.

The mechanics

A side income that outgrows its current capacity has exactly three real levers available to resolve the gap, and "work harder" isn't one of them — it's the absence of a decision, not a real option, because it borrows against your health and your primary job in a way that eventually collapses under its own weight, as it does for the technician in this chapter's opening. The three legitimate levers are: raise prices to reduce demand to a level that fits your current capacity, increase capacity through better tools or process without adding hours, or add help — a subcontractor, a part-time assistant, or a specific outsourced task — to genuinely expand what a fixed number of your own hours can produce.

Each lever solves a genuinely different problem, and choosing the wrong one for your specific situation is a common and costly mistake. Raising prices is the correct lever when demand exceeds capacity and the work itself is already about as efficient as it can reasonably get — it doesn't increase your hours, but it reduces the number of clients competing for them, and it increases what you earn per hour of the capacity you do have. Increasing capacity through better process or tools is the correct lever when real inefficiency exists in how the work currently gets done — time lost to manual scheduling, redundant communication, or a workflow that hasn't been streamlined since the earliest, smallest version of the business. Adding help is the correct lever when the work itself is efficient and correctly priced, but there simply aren't enough hours in your own week to meet real demand, and specific pieces of the work can reasonably be delegated without compromising the quality that built the demand in the first place.

The mistake most people make at this stage is reaching for the lever that feels least uncomfortable rather than the one that actually matches the problem — raising prices feels uncomfortable because it risks losing clients, so people avoid it even when it's clearly the right tool; adding help feels risky and complicated, so people avoid it even when the work genuinely has delegable pieces; and "just work harder" feels like the safest, least confrontational choice of all, even though it's reliably the one that produces burnout and declining quality, exactly as it does in this chapter's opening scenario.

It's worth being precise about why "just work harder" feels safe even though it's structurally the riskiest of the four options. Raising prices, improving process, and delegating all involve a visible, external moment of risk — a client might say no, a tool might not deliver the expected savings, a delegate might not meet the bar. Working harder involves no external risk at all; the only cost is internal, paid quietly out of your own hours and energy rather than surfaced in a single visible moment where something could go wrong. That asymmetry in visible-versus-invisible risk is exactly why it gets chosen so often despite being the worst option on the list — the cost is real, but it's deferred and diffuse rather than immediate and specific, which makes it easy to underweight until it's already produced the kind of decline this chapter's opening describes.

The script and framework

Step 1 — Diagnose the actual gap before choosing a lever. Is demand simply higher than any reasonable capacity could meet (a pricing problem)? Is the work itself taking longer than it should because of inefficient process (a capacity problem)? Or is the work efficient and correctly priced, but genuinely too much for one person's available hours (a delegation problem)? Be honest here — these three diagnoses call for different fixes, and applying the wrong one wastes real time and can make the underlying strain worse.

Step 2 — If it's a pricing problem, raise prices deliberately, using the confidence-building evidence you've accumulated since Chapter 3. By this stage, you have real proof — a track record of satisfied clients, specific results — that your Chapter 3 introductory pricing never had. A price increase framed around that real evidence, applied to new clients first and existing clients with reasonable notice, is a legitimate, expected part of a growing business, not something that requires an apology.

Step 3 — If it's a capacity problem, audit your actual process for the specific step consuming disproportionate time, and fix that step specifically rather than trying to work faster across the board. A scheduling tool, a standard client-intake form that collects information up front instead of over several back-and-forth messages, a template that replaces a document built from scratch each time — small, specific process fixes frequently recover meaningful hours without touching the quality of the work itself.

Step 4 — If it's a delegation problem, identify the specific, delegable piece of the work first, rather than looking for a general assistant. What part of the process doesn't require your specific skill — editing, scheduling, basic client communication, administrative tasks — and could be handled by someone else without compromising the part of the work that's actually yours. Start with a narrow, specific delegation rather than a broad hire, both because it's lower-risk and because it's easier to evaluate whether it worked.

Step 5 — Reassess your Chapter 5 hour ceiling and Chapter 8 allocation split every time you apply one of these levers. Scaling changes the underlying numbers this book already gave you tools for — a lever that increases revenue per hour or effectively adds hours through delegation should prompt a fresh look at both your time boundaries and your reinvest-versus-pay-yourself split, rather than leaving either one fixed at its original, earlier-stage setting indefinitely.

It's worth noticing that these five steps loop rather than run once and finish — a business that resolves a capacity gap through one lever frequently grows into a new, larger version of the same gap eventually, simply at a bigger scale. That's not a sign the fix failed; it's the normal shape of a genuinely growing side income, and the correct response each time is the same diagnostic process from Step 1, run fresh against the new situation, rather than assuming last time's lever automatically applies again.

Worked example

The pet photographer diagnoses her situation honestly: her booking and editing process is reasonably efficient already, and the demand genuinely exceeds what her existing hour ceiling can support — a pricing and, secondarily, a light delegation problem, not a process problem. She raises her session price by 30 percent for all new bookings, using her now-substantial portfolio of finished work and a stack of specific client testimonials as visible, unspoken justification rather than anything she needs to explain defensively.

The price increase reduces new inquiries by roughly a third, which brings demand back in line with her available hours without her needing to work a single additional evening. For the remaining gap, she identifies photo editing — not the actual shoot, which requires her specific skill and presence, but the post-processing afterward — as a genuinely delegable piece of the work, and hires a part-time freelance photo editor for eight hours a month to handle a portion of it, a narrow, specific delegation rather than a broad, risky hire. Both moves together restore her hour ceiling to a sustainable range, and her actual full-time job's performance, which had started slipping under the earlier "just work harder" approach, recovers within a month.

A second worked example

A church choir director who teaches private voice lessons on the side runs into a version of this chapter's problem that looks different from a straightforward demand surge: her calendar is full, but her actual revenue per hour has stayed flat for two years, even as her reputation and waitlist have both grown considerably. Diagnosing the gap, she realizes it isn't a capacity problem at all — she has more demand than she can serve, which normally points toward pricing, but she's been reluctant to raise her rate because several of her longest-standing students are on modest, fixed budgets and she doesn't want to price them out.

Rather than a blanket price increase, which is the standard lever but not a comfortable fit for her specific situation, she applies a tiered version of it: new students are quoted at a meaningfully higher rate, reflecting her now-substantial waitlist and reputation, while her existing long-term students are grandfathered at their current rate with an honest, direct note that new students are being quoted higher given demand. This resolves her actual capacity math — new students at the higher rate fill her few remaining open slots faster, cooling the waitlist pressure without a single existing relationship being disrupted — while sidestepping the specific discomfort a blanket increase would have created for her. It's a reminder that the three levers in this chapter aren't always applied uniformly across an entire client base; a segmented application of the same underlying lever is often the better fit once real relationships and real history are part of the picture.

Common objections and how to handle them

"What if raising prices loses me most of my client base?" A price increase applied thoughtfully — to new clients first, with reasonable advance notice to existing ones, and grounded in real, demonstrated proof of value — rarely produces the mass exodus people fear. Some attrition at the margin is normal and, in a genuine demand-exceeds-capacity situation, is actually part of the intended effect: losing your least profitable or least ideal clients to a price increase while keeping the ones who value the work most is the mechanism working correctly, not a failure of it.

"What if I can't afford to hire anyone, even part-time?" Delegation doesn't require a formal employee relationship. A narrow, specific task handed to a freelance contractor for a fixed, small number of hours a month — as the photographer did with her editor — is a low-commitment way to test whether delegation actually helps before considering anything larger or more permanent. Start with the smallest viable version of the delegation, evaluate it against the same specific-expectation discipline from Chapter 8's reinvestment framework, and expand only once it's proven itself.

"What if none of the three levers seem to fit my situation?" Revisit the diagnosis in Step 1 more carefully — in practice, nearly every capacity problem resolves into some combination of the three, even when it doesn't look that way at first. A situation that feels unsolvable is often actually a pricing problem wearing a process-problem disguise, or a process problem being misread as a need for help. Walk through all three diagnostic questions explicitly, in writing, rather than relying on a general impression of being "too busy," which tends to obscure which specific lever the situation actually calls for.

Frequently misunderstood point: scaling isn't always the right goal

This chapter assumes growth is the objective once demand exceeds capacity, but it's worth saying plainly that staying at your current size, on purpose, is a completely legitimate choice too — not every side income needs to keep expanding just because it can. If the current size of the business already fits comfortably inside the hour ceiling from Chapter 5 and produces the income you actually want from it, the correct response to excess demand can simply be a longer waitlist and a polite no to the overflow, rather than reaching for one of the three levers by default. Scaling exists as a set of tools for when growth is genuinely wanted — it isn't an obligation that kicks in automatically the moment demand outpaces the business's current size.

A note on saying no without damaging the relationship

Not every capacity gap needs one of the three structural levers — sometimes the right answer, for a specific request, is simply a clear, polite no, without a fee increase or a hire attached to it. A useful, low-friction way to decline a specific request that exceeds your current capacity: "I'd love to help with this, but I'm at capacity through [specific date] — I can either put you on my list for after that, or point you toward someone else if the timing doesn't work for you." This keeps the relationship intact, gives the requester real options, and avoids the trap of saying yes to demand your actual capacity can't support, which is exactly the pattern that produced the photographer's burnout in this chapter's opening.

A full conversation, start to finish

The choir director's tiered pricing decision, played out in a real exchange with a prospective new student.

Prospective student's parent: "I heard you have a waitlist, but wondered if there's any way to get my daughter in sooner?"

Choir director: "I do have a short waitlist right now given demand — for new students, my rate is $75 a lesson, which reflects where things are at currently. If that works, I can likely get her started within the next few weeks rather than the full waitlist wait."

Parent: "That's more than I expected, but if it means she can start sooner, that's worth it to us."

Choir director: "Great — I'll follow up with some open slot times this week."

Notice what doesn't happen here: no apology for the higher new-student rate, no lengthy justification volunteered before it was asked for, and no attempt to quietly match her long-standing students' older, lower rate out of discomfort with the gap between the two. The rate is stated plainly, the benefit — a shorter wait — is stated alongside it, and the conversation moves forward. This is the same evidence-backed, plainly delivered confidence the very first chapter of this book's companion negotiation volume teaches, applied here to a pricing lever rather than a negotiation.

A short exercise before you move to Chapter 10

Run the three-question diagnosis from Step 1 against your own current capacity situation, even if it doesn't yet feel urgent. Write down which of the three levers — pricing, process, or delegation — most honestly matches what you're seeing, and identify one small, specific first move for that lever you could make within the next two weeks. Scaling problems tend to compound quietly before they become obvious, and diagnosing the gap early, before it forces itself on you the way it did on the photographer, is what keeps the fix small and manageable instead of a full-blown crisis.

Recognizing burnout before it costs you the primary job

The three levers in this chapter exist to prevent the outcome the photographer experienced in this chapter's opening, but it's worth being explicit about what early burnout actually looks like, since it rarely announces itself as clearly as "I am now burned out." It tends to show up first as small, easy-to-dismiss signals: a growing reluctance to open side-income messages that used to feel exciting, a shortening temper with people close to you that has nothing to do with anything they've done, a specific and unusual number of small mistakes at your primary job clustered into a short window, or physical signs — poor sleep, skipped meals, a persistent low-grade exhaustion — that don't resolve with a normal weekend of rest.

None of these signals, individually, proves burnout is underway. Together, and especially if they've appeared since a period of rising side-income demand, they're worth treating as seriously as the diagnostic questions in Step 1 — because a side income that's technically thriving on paper while quietly damaging your health or your primary job's performance isn't a success by this book's own standard. The honest response, when these signals cluster, is the same one available throughout this book: a temporary, deliberate reduction in scope — a smaller hour ceiling from Chapter 5, a firmer no to new demand, or one of this chapter's three levers applied specifically to reduce the current load rather than to grow it — until the signals resolve. Scaling a business you've burned yourself out of is not actually scaling; it's borrowing against a future you haven't budgeted for.

Knowing when a specific scaling decision didn't work

Not every application of the three levers in this chapter succeeds on the first attempt, and it's worth having a clear way to evaluate whether a specific move actually worked rather than assuming it did simply because it's now in place. A price increase that produces no meaningful reduction in demand and no meaningful increase in per-hour earnings — because it wasn't set high enough, or because the underlying value proposition didn't support it — hasn't resolved the capacity problem it was meant to address. A process fix that saves less time than expected, once measured honestly against the specific expectation set before adopting it, is worth reversing or replacing rather than keeping out of sunk-cost attachment to the tool itself. A delegated task that requires more oversight than it saves in actual hours has produced a net loss, not a net gain, however uncomfortable it feels to acknowledge that after already investing in setting it up.

The discipline here mirrors Chapter 8's reinvestment evaluation directly: set a specific, measurable expectation before applying any lever, and check the real result against it a set number of weeks later, honestly, rather than assuming success by default because the change is now in place. A scaling lever that isn't working is worth correcting quickly — the cost of reversing a bad fix early is far lower than the cost of running an ineffective one for months while the underlying capacity problem continues, unresolved, underneath it.

Scaling as an ongoing discipline, not a one-time fix

It's worth closing this chapter by naming the pattern underneath all three levers: capacity problems in a growing side income aren't a single hurdle to clear once and move past permanently — they're a recurring feature of any business that keeps growing, showing up again at a larger scale each time the previous gap gets resolved. The choir director's tiered pricing, the photographer's combined price increase and light delegation, the veterinary technician turned mobile photographer managing her own hour ceiling — none of these are one-time fixes so much as the first application of a diagnostic habit that will need running again, at a bigger scale, as the business continues to grow.

Treat this chapter's three-question diagnosis as a tool to revisit periodically, not a problem to solve once and file away. A brief, honest capacity check — every quarter, or whenever demand noticeably shifts — keeps the gap between demand and capacity from ever growing large enough to force the kind of crisis-mode reaction that opened this chapter. Growth handled this way, in small, deliberate corrections applied early, feels almost unremarkable from the inside — which is exactly the point, since the alternative, handled reactively and late, is the burnout this chapter exists to prevent.

Chapter 10 — The Honest Math of Replacing a Primary Income

When a side income can realistically become the whole thing, and when it can't

The situation

A city bus driver's furniture-flipping and reselling side business, three years in, is generating a genuinely impressive $3,200 a month in gross revenue — more than half of his take-home pay from driving. Friends and family, seeing the number, start suggesting he quit driving and go all-in. He's seriously tempted. What nobody in his life is doing, including him, is running the actual math on what that $3,200 in gross side-business revenue really translates to once it's the only income supporting his household, rather than a supplement sitting on top of a stable primary paycheck.

The mechanics

The single most common error in deciding whether a side income can replace a primary income is comparing the wrong two numbers: side-business gross revenue against primary-job take-home pay. These aren't comparable figures, and the gap between them is usually much larger than it first appears, for reasons that have nothing to do with whether the side business is actually good.

First, gross revenue isn't profit. Materials, tools, mileage, marketplace fees, and the tax set-aside from Chapter 7 all come out of that $3,200 before any of it is genuinely available to live on — and once self-employment tax is added on top of ordinary income tax, the real, spendable amount is meaningfully lower than the headline figure suggests.

Second, a primary job's compensation is rarely just the paycheck. Health insurance, retirement matching, paid time off, disability coverage, and other benefits all have a real dollar value that has to be replaced, out of pocket, the moment a primary job is gone — and self-purchased versions of the same coverage are almost always more expensive than an employer-subsidized version, sometimes dramatically so. A side income that appears to match a primary job's take-home pay on paper frequently doesn't match it at all once these replacement costs are added into the comparison honestly.

Third, and perhaps most overlooked: a side income's revenue, earned in spare hours alongside a stable job, behaves very differently once it becomes the sole source of household income and the sole demand on all of your working hours. Some of that difference is positive — full-time hours applied to a business that was previously squeezed into evenings can genuinely grow revenue. But some of it is real risk that a side-income comparison doesn't capture: income volatility that was easily absorbed by a stable primary paycheck becomes existential once there's no paycheck underneath it, and the psychological and practical pressure of needing every month's revenue to cover the mortgage, rather than needing it to cover discretionary spending, changes the entire risk profile of running the business.

None of this means a side income can never become a full replacement — it demonstrably can, and does, for real people running real businesses. It means the decision deserves an honest, specific calculation rather than a comparison of two mismatched numbers, and it means the transition, when it's genuinely warranted, usually goes better as a deliberate, staged process than as a single leap made on the strength of one especially good month.

There's a final mechanical point worth making explicit, because it changes how the whole calculation should be read: a side income and a primary job aren't actually being compared as though they're interchangeable versions of the same thing. A primary job trades a fixed, predictable number of hours for a fixed, predictable paycheck and a bundle of benefits. A side income scaled to full-time hours trades a variable, self-directed number of hours for a variable, self-generated income with no guaranteed floor. The honest math in this chapter isn't just converting one number into a comparable version of the other — it's making the underlying risk difference visible enough to actually weigh, rather than letting an exciting revenue figure obscure the fact that the two arrangements carry fundamentally different kinds of certainty.

The script and framework

Step 1 — Calculate your true replacement number, not your current take-home pay. Add your primary job's take-home pay to the real annual cost of replacing every benefit you'd lose — health insurance premiums at an individual market rate, the value of any employer retirement match, an honest estimate of paid time off's value, and any other benefit that has a real replacement cost. This total, not your paycheck alone, is the number your side income actually needs to clear.

Step 2 — Calculate your side income's true net, not its gross. Subtract real business expenses and your full tax set-aside — remembering that self-employment tax applies to the full amount once it's your sole income, not just the supplemental amount it was before — to find what the business genuinely nets you per month, on average, across at least six to twelve months of real data rather than a single strong month.

Step 3 — Build a volatility-adjusted average, not a best-month average. Look at your worst three months over the available track record, not your best three. A side income that averages $3,200 a month but has swung between $900 and $5,500 across its history carries meaningfully more risk as a sole income than one that's averaged the same $3,200 with much tighter month-to-month variation — and that risk should directly shape how much runway you build before making any transition.

Step 4 — Build a specific runway before transitioning, sized to your calculated volatility. A commonly used starting point is six to twelve months of full living expenses in accessible savings before leaving a primary job for a side income that's shown real but variable revenue — longer for a highly volatile business, shorter for one with unusually stable, contract-based revenue. This runway exists specifically to absorb the worst-month scenario from Step 3 without financial crisis while the business continues operating at full-time capacity.

Step 5 — Where possible, stage the transition rather than making it a single leap. Reducing primary-job hours gradually if your employer allows it, or setting a specific, evidence-based trigger (a specific number of consecutive months clearing your true replacement number from Step 1, not just a single strong month) before making a full transition, meaningfully reduces the risk of the decision compared to quitting on the strength of one exceptional month that later proves to be an outlier rather than a new normal.

Run all five steps in writing, on paper or in a document you keep and revisit, rather than as a mental estimate. The true replacement number, the true net, the volatility-adjusted average, the runway target, and the staging plan belong together in one place, updated every time you revisit the decision, so the whole calculation is available to review as a single, coherent picture rather than five separate impressions held loosely in memory and prone to drifting optimistic exactly when the excitement of a strong month makes optimism most tempting.

Worked example

The bus driver runs the actual numbers rather than relying on the encouraging general impression his $3,200 gross revenue had created. His true replacement number: his current take-home pay, plus an estimated $650 a month to replace his employer health coverage at individual-market rates, plus the value of his retirement match, plus a conservative estimate for lost paid time off — a total meaningfully higher than his simple take-home pay alone.

His side business's true net, after materials, marketplace fees, mileage, and his full self-employment tax set-aside, comes to roughly $2,100 a month on average — well below the $3,200 gross figure that had generated the original excitement, and well below his true replacement number once benefits are factored in. His worst three months over the past two years, rather than his best, average closer to $1,400, revealing more real volatility in the business than the encouraging average had suggested. Rather than quitting immediately, he sets a specific trigger: six consecutive months clearing his full true replacement number, plus nine months of expenses saved as runway, before making the transition. He also asks his employer about reducing to part-time driving hours as an interim step, which they accommodate, giving him more hours for the furniture business while keeping a partial income and partial benefits intact during the buildup. The transition, when it eventually happens fourteen months later, happens on the strength of real, sustained numbers rather than one especially good month — the honest math this chapter exists to walk through, run all the way to its actual conclusion.

A second worked example

A hotel concierge with a growing side business offering personalized local-experience planning for visitors — an offer built directly on the specific knowledge and relationships she developed over a decade at the front desk — runs her own version of this chapter's math after a magazine feature drives a temporary surge in bookings. Her gross revenue that month is her best ever, more than double her usual pace, and it's tempting to treat it as proof the business has fully arrived.

She resists the temptation and runs the full calculation instead. Her true replacement number includes her hotel's health coverage, a modest retirement contribution match she'd otherwise lose, and the steady, predictable nature of a bi-weekly paycheck that her seasonal, feature-driven side business doesn't currently replicate. Looking at her worst three months over the past eighteen months rather than the magazine-feature month, her volatility-adjusted true net comes in well below her replacement number — the feature-driven spike was real, but it wasn't representative, and treating it as the new baseline would have meant transitioning off a number that was never going to repeat reliably. She sets her trigger at six consecutive typical months — deliberately excluding any future one-time press spikes from the qualifying average — clearing her true replacement number, and keeps working her hotel job through two more slow seasons before the business's baseline, not just its occasional peak, genuinely earns the transition.

Common objections and how to handle them

"What if I can never save a full runway before I'd want to make the transition?" A full six-to-twelve-month runway is a strong, conservative target, not the only responsible path. A partial transition — reduced primary-job hours, as the driver's employer accommodated, or a spouse's or partner's income covering a larger share of fixed expenses during a buildup period — can responsibly substitute for part of a full cash runway, provided the volatility math from Step 3 is still run honestly against whatever safety net actually exists. What matters is that some real plan for absorbing a bad-month scenario exists before the transition, not that the plan takes one specific form.

"What if my side income's true net already clearly exceeds my true replacement number?" Then the math in this chapter has done its job, and the remaining decision is about risk tolerance and timing rather than whether the transition is mathematically sound. Even in a clearly favorable case, running the volatility check in Step 3 and building at least some runway remains worthwhile — a business that comfortably clears its replacement number on average can still have a genuinely bad quarter, and a transition made without any buffer at all treats an average as a guarantee it was never meant to be.

"Isn't all this caution just another way of talking myself out of ever making the leap?" The honest math in this chapter isn't built to produce a no — plenty of side incomes clear it comfortably and the transition goes well, which is the entire reason the framework exists rather than a blanket recommendation to never leave a primary job. What it's built to prevent is a transition made on the strength of a single strong month, compared against the wrong baseline number, without any plan for the inevitable slow stretch that follows even a genuinely successful business. Following the framework and getting a clear yes is just as real an outcome as getting a not-yet.

Frequently misunderstood point: a strong single month is a data point, not a trend

The single most expensive mistake this chapter guards against isn't a math error — it's a timing error, specifically the temptation to run the replacement calculation right after an unusually good month and mistake that month's number for the business's real, ongoing baseline. Both the bus driver's and the concierge's worked examples hinge on exactly this distinction: a strong month is genuinely worth celebrating and genuinely worth learning from, but it earns a place in the volatility-adjusted average from Step 3, not a promotion to the number the whole transition decision gets built around. The businesses in both examples were real and were working — the mistake being avoided wasn't optimism about the business, it was mistaking its ceiling for its floor.

A note on partial transitions as a permanent arrangement, not just a phase

Not every side income needs to become a full replacement to be worth continuing, and it's worth saying plainly that a permanently part-time arrangement — reduced primary-job hours indefinitely, or a side income that simply stays a meaningful supplemental income stream for years — is a completely legitimate outcome of everything in this book, not a consolation prize for a transition that didn't happen. The honest math in this chapter exists to inform a real decision, and "the numbers say stay partial, and that's genuinely fine" is as valid a conclusion as "the numbers say go all in."

Warning signs the transition is being rushed

A short list worth checking against your own situation before making any final decision, since these patterns show up across very different businesses and professions. You're calculating your replacement number using take-home pay alone, without adding back the real cost of lost benefits — that's the exact mismatched comparison this chapter opens with. You're using your best month, or a recent unusual spike, as your baseline rather than a genuine average across a longer stretch — that's the timing error the previous section addresses directly. You haven't built any runway at all, on the theory that the business's current momentum will simply carry through any rough patch — that's optimism standing in for a plan. And you're avoiding the actual calculation altogether, relying instead on a general feeling that "it's probably fine by now" — which is understandable, because the feeling of being ready is genuinely exciting, but it's exactly the feeling this chapter's arithmetic exists to check against reality rather than replace.

A short exercise before you close this book

Calculate your own true replacement number and your side income's volatility-adjusted true net, using your real numbers rather than a hopeful estimate, even if a full transition feels far off right now. Write both figures down, along with the gap between them, and revisit the calculation every six months as your side income develops. This exercise, done honestly and repeated on a schedule, is what turns "maybe someday" into an actual, evidence-based decision whenever the numbers genuinely support it — which is the same principle behind every framework in this book, applied one last time to the biggest decision it covers.

Building a transition plan you can actually execute

Once the math in this chapter genuinely supports a transition, it's worth converting the decision from a calculation into a short, written plan — the same discipline this book has applied to every other major decision, from the skill inventory in Chapter 1 to the allocation split in Chapter 8. A usable transition plan answers five questions in one place: what is the specific trigger that's now been met (the exact numbers, not a general sense of readiness); what is the actual notice period and process for leaving or reducing the primary job, including any benefits continuation window worth understanding in advance; what does the runway cover, specifically, and for how many months at current expenses; is the transition happening in a single step or a staged one, and if staged, what's the next specific milestone; and who, if anyone, needs to be told, and on what timeline, so the transition doesn't happen in a rush once the decision is made.

Writing this plan down before acting on it serves the same purpose every written trigger and checklist in this book has served: it separates the moment of excitement about a strong month from the moment of actual action, inserting a deliberate pause where the full picture — replacement number, true net, volatility, runway — gets reviewed one final time before anything irreversible happens. A transition made from a written plan, reviewed calmly, is a fundamentally different decision than one made in the excitement of a single good week, even when the underlying numbers are identical.

What happens after the transition, in the first year

It's worth setting honest expectations for the year immediately following a genuine transition, since even a well-prepared move rarely feels as settled as the spreadsheet made it look in advance. The most common adjustment is psychological rather than financial: income that once arrived alongside a stable paycheck, functioning as a bonus on top of a known floor, now has to function as the entire floor itself, and that shift in role changes how the same numbers feel even when they match the plan exactly. Revenue that once felt like exciting extra money can start to feel like pressure once nothing else is backstopping it, and it's worth expecting that adjustment rather than reading it as a sign the transition was a mistake.

It's also worth revisiting the tax and structure decisions from Chapters 6 and 7 within the first few months of a full transition, since self-employment tax now applies to the entire household income rather than a supplemental portion, and the liability checklist from Chapter 6 deserves a fresh look now that the business is the sole source of support rather than a side venture with a safety net underneath it. Treat the first full year post-transition as its own distinct season, worth its own honest review at the twelve-month mark — not to second-guess a decision that was made on real, evidence-based math, but to make sure the structure supporting the business has kept pace with what the business has become.

Closing

Go back to the gate agent from Chapter 7, the paralegal from Chapter 6, the teacher from Chapter 1. None of them started this book with an unusual skill. What they had, once they finished building the systems in these chapters, wasn't a different talent — it was a structure their talent could finally run inside of: an offer specific enough for a stranger to say yes to, a price grounded in real research instead of a guess, a first client found through a warm list and a direct ask instead of an ad budget nobody had, hours protected clearly enough that a full-time job never had to pay the price for a side project's growth, and paperwork handled early and calmly enough that April never became a crisis.

That's the actual difference between a skill that stays a favor people ask for free, indefinitely, and a skill that becomes a second income stream showing up on a real schedule. It was never about wanting it more. It was about mechanics — the offer, the price, the outreach, the boundary, the tax set-aside, the honest math — each one a decision you can make correctly on your own numbers, in your own situation, without needing anyone's permission or a story about how someone else finally made theirs work.

None of the ten chapters in this book requires the others to be finished first, and none of them requires a dramatic leap of faith to start. Most start with fifteen minutes and a piece of paper — the raw skill list from Chapter 1, the warm-contact list from Chapter 4, the cost-plus floor from Chapter 3. The distance between having a skill people already ask you for and having a second income stream that shows up reliably isn't talent, and it isn't luck. It's the specific, ordinary mechanics this book spent ten chapters walking through, one decision at a time, in an order that holds up regardless of which skill, which schedule, or which primary job you're building around. Pick the chapter that matches where you actually are, do the exercise at the end of it this week, and let the next chapter wait until the one before it is genuinely done. That's the whole method, and it's the same one every side income in this book was built with, one ordinary decision at a time.

The furniture builder from Chapter 4 is still driving a forklift. So is the bus driver from Chapter 10, at least for now, on his own deliberate timeline rather than anyone else's. That's not a lesser outcome than a dramatic career pivot — it's the point. A second income stream doesn't require abandoning the first one to prove it was worth building. It requires a system that runs alongside it, on its own schedule, until the numbers, not the excitement of a good month, say it's ready to become something more. Whatever skill you're sitting on right now, the next step isn't a leap. It's fifteen minutes and a piece of paper, and Chapter 1 is exactly where to start.

Notes & Further Reading

This book draws on real, verifiable government and institutional sources for its tax and business-structure guidance, and deliberately avoids citing specific dollar thresholds, tax rates, or filing fees as fixed facts, since these are set and periodically adjusted by federal and state authorities and should always be confirmed directly before acting.

- **IRS Publication 334, Tax Guide for Small Business** — the foundational IRS guide for sole proprietors, covering what counts as self-employment income, deductible business expenses, and recordkeeping. Available at irs.gov. - **IRS Publication 505, Tax Withholding and Estimated Tax**, and **Form 1040-ES** — the official guidance and worksheet for calculating and paying quarterly estimated taxes, including the safe-harbor rules referenced in Chapter 7. Available at irs.gov. - **IRS Schedule SE (Form 1040), Self-Employment Tax** — the official form and instructions covering how self-employment tax is calculated, including current rates. Available at irs.gov. - **IRS Schedule C (Form 1040), Profit or Loss From Business** — the official form for reporting sole-proprietorship income and expenses, with instructions detailing which business expenses are deductible. Available at irs.gov. - **U.S. Small Business Administration — "Choose a Business Structure"** (sba.gov) — federal guidance comparing sole proprietorships, LLCs, partnerships, and corporations, including liability and tax implications of each. - **U.S. Small Business Administration — "Calculate Your Startup Costs"** and related SBA small-business planning guidance (sba.gov) — federal resources on early-stage business financial planning referenced in the reinvestment framework in Chapter 8. - **U.S. Bureau of Labor Statistics — Contingent Worker Supplement, Current Population Survey** (bls.gov) — the federal government's periodic survey data on independent contractors, gig work, and supplemental income arrangements in the U.S. labor force, relevant background for the broader side-income landscape this book addresses. - **U.S. Bureau of Labor Statistics — Occupational Employment and Wage Statistics** (bls.gov) — federal wage data by occupation, a legitimate starting reference point for the comparable-market pricing research described in Chapter 3, alongside direct industry research specific to your own field. - **IRS Form SS-8, Determination of Worker Status** and related IRS worker-classification guidance (irs.gov) — the federal framework for distinguishing an employee from an independent contractor, referenced in Chapter 6's discussion of bringing on a first subcontractor. - **U.S. Small Business Administration — Small Business Development Centers (SBDC) network** (sba.gov) — a federally supported, no-cost or low-cost local business advising resource, referenced in Chapter 6 as a starting point for questions specific to an individual's business risk profile or entity structure. - **The curse of knowledge** — the cognitive bias, referenced in Chapter 1, in which a person who has mastered a skill loses easy access to what it felt like not to know it, making the skill harder to recognize as sellable. Originally described in Camerer, Loewenstein, and Weber, "The Curse of Knowledge in Economic Settings: An Experimental Analysis," *Journal of Political Economy*, 1989. - **IRS Small Business and Self-Employed Tax Center** (irs.gov) — the IRS's central hub for self-employment tax topics, recordkeeping requirements, and links to the specific forms and publications referenced throughout Chapters 6 through 8 of this book.

Readers should verify all current tax rates, filing thresholds, safe-harbor percentages, and state-specific LLC formation requirements directly with the IRS, the SBA, and their own state's business-filing agency before acting, since this book's role is to explain the underlying mechanics rather than to serve as a substitute for current, jurisdiction-specific guidance from a licensed tax professional or attorney.

A final note on scope: this book focuses on U.S. federal tax and business-structure mechanics specifically, since that's the framework its worked examples and its Notes are built against. Readers outside the United States will find the underlying logic — separating a skill from an offer, pricing a first sale, protecting a primary job's hours, deciding when a side income can responsibly replace a primary one — fully transferable, but should substitute their own country's tax authority, business-registration requirements, and self-employment obligations for the specific U.S. sources listed above.

About

The Side Income Playbook is part of the Wealth Mechanics library — a series covering the concrete, learnable mechanics behind everyday money decisions: negotiation, debt payoff, pricing, automated saving systems, savings rate, investment onboarding, and, in this volume, the specific mechanical steps behind turning an existing skill into a real second income stream without leaving a primary job. Where some books explore the psychology behind why money decisions feel hard, Wealth Mechanics stays entirely in the mechanics: what to actually do, in what order, and why each step is built the way it is.

Daniel Cross writes the Wealth Mechanics series. His approach is shaped by years spent building financial systems for people who already knew what they should be doing and needed a structure that didn't depend on remembering to do it — the same principle behind every book in this library, applied here to the specific mechanics of building income rather than managing it.

Readers of this volume who found the tactical, script-driven approach useful may also want *The Pricing Playbook*, which covers pricing mechanics for an already-established freelance or service business, and *The Negotiation Playbook*, which covers the broader skill of money conversations — salary, rate, and contract negotiation — that a growing side income eventually needs as client relationships and their terms mature.

Also in the Series

Every book in Wealth Mechanics stands on its own — read them in any order. If this one was useful, the library continues:

The Negotiation Playbook

The Debt Freedom System

The Pricing Playbook

The Automatic Wealth System

The Savings Rate Playbook

The Investment Onboarding Playbook

The Real Estate Entry Playbook

The Tax Reduction Playbook

The Equity Compensation Playbook